JAMES JOYCE
& the
BURDEN
OF DISEASE

JAMES JOYCE
& THE
BURDEN
OF DISEASE

Kathleen Ferris

THE UNIVERSITY PRESS OF KENTUCKY

Frontispiece: Photograph of James Joyce courtesy of the
Beinecke Rare Book and Manuscript Library,
Yale University Library.

Copyright © 1995 by The University Press of Kentucky

Scholarly publisher for the Commonwealth,
serving Bellarmine College, Berea College, Centre
College of Kentucky, Eastern Kentucky University,
The Filson Club, Georgetown College, Kentucky
Historical Society, Kentucky State University,
Morehead State University, Murray State University,
Northern Kentucky University, Transylvania University,
University of Kentucky, University of Louisville,
and Western Kentucky University
Editorial and Sales Offices: Lexington, Kentucky 40508-4008

Library of Congress Cataloging-in-Publication Data

Ferris, Kathleen, 1941-
    James Joyce and the burden of disease / Kathleen Ferris.
        p.   cm.
    Includes bibliographical references (p.) and index.
    ISBN 0-8131-1893-X:
    1. Joyce, James, 1882-1941—Health. 2. Novelists, Irish—20th
century—Biography. 3. Syphilis—Patients—Ireland—Biography.
4. Venereal diseases in literature. 5. Body, Human, in literature.
6. Syphilis in literature. 7. Health in literature. I. Title.
PR6019.09Z533378 1994
823'.912—dc20
[B]   94-19905

This book is printed on acid-free recycled paper meeting
the requirements of the American National Standard
for Permanence of Paper for Printed Library Materials. ♾ ♺

Contents

Illustrations

Acknowledgments

First, my thanks to Oliver D. Gogarty, son of Oliver St. John Gogarty, for his consent to my quoting from the letters of his father; to Erwin Ellmann, brother of Richard Ellmann, for his permission to quote from the Ellmann correspondence and interviews; to Margaret Gibson Phillips, daughter of Desmond Harmsworth, for permission to reproduce the sketch "Joyce at Midnight"; and to the Board of Trinity College, Dublin, for permission to reproduce two images from *The Book of Kells*. Thanks also to Yale University Library for authorizing use of manuscript materials and the photograph of Joyce that appears on the dust jacket, all of which are located in the Beinecke Rare Book and Manuscript Library; to the Harry Ransom Humanities Research Center for permission to use the sketch "Joyce at Midnight"; to The Poetry/Rare Books Collection, University Libraries, State University of New York at Buffalo for permission to cite manuscripts; and to the Cornell University Library for permission to cite manuscripts from the Division of Rare and Manuscripts Collections.

Further, I wish to express my debt to the many people whose assistance and encouragement have made this book possible:

First, my gratitude to three eminent Joyceans who gave very generously of their time to read and critique the manuscript in its earlier stages. Morton Levitt, Fritz Senn, and the late Bernard Benstock offered corrections, advice, and criticisms that have helped me to strengthen my argument and have, I hope, saved me from future embarrassment. Whereas I am deeply indebted to them all, I claim all remaining deficiencies of the book as my own.

Also I wish to thank the medical doctors who have given

so much of their time, expertise, and library resources to help me understand the complexities of fields of study not my own. My opthalmologist, Dr. Harold Akin, spent many hours reviewing the medical and literary evidence with me, and without his assistance and encouragement I might have abandoned this project in its early stages. Dr. Frank Carter, an internist, twice read my third chapter to check the medical information, as did Dr. Harold Akin and Dr. J. Howard Young, my gynecologist. The late Dr. Rudolph Kampmeier kindly spent an afternoon reviewing my evidence and explaining to me the symptoms and cycles of a disease that he had spent many years of his life treating before the advent of penicillin. Dr. Hansreudi Isler listened to my ideas and tried to assist me from Zurich. Psychologist Richard L. Saylor, who works with schizophrenics, discussed with me the manifestations of that disease and provided me with valuable literature. Drs. Mark Simpson, Howard Simpson, Robert Sanders, and Harold Akin also lent me textbooks from which I launched my medical study.

My doctoral committee at Emory University played a crucial role in the early stages of this endeavor. My director, Dr. Ronald Schuchard, gave me encouragement and, perhaps more important, the freedom to follow my own ideas, providing his knowledge of Joyce and Joycean scholarship to guide me. Dr. James Flannery, with his broad knowledge of Ireland and of the literature of the period, gave my work close critical reading and offered me invaluable advice on how to get it published. Dr. Georgia Christopher was a careful editor who played the Devil's Advocate with a vengeance.

My school, Lincoln Memorial University, and the Faculty Scholars Program at the University of Kentucky enabled me to attend Joyce conferences, thus providing me the opportunity to present my ideas to a forum of Joyce scholars.

Librarians at many schools have given me kindly assistance, for which I am very grateful: Dr. Thomas Staley, Research Librarian Cathy Henderson, and Barbara LaBorde at the Harry Ransom Humanities Research Center of the University

of Texas at Austin; Mr. Sidney F. Huttner and his staff at the
McFarlin Library of the University of Tulsa; James Tyler, Lucy
Burgess, and Elaine Engst at the Division of Rare and Manu-
script Collections of Cornell University; Dr. Robert Bertholf
and his staff at The Poetry/Rare Books Collection, University
Libraries, State University of New York at Buffalo; and Doris
Dysinger and her staff in Special Collections at Bucknell
University. Also the interlibrary loan departments at Emory
University (Margaret Whittier), Middle Tennessee State University (Almyra Medlin and Betty McFall), and Lincoln Memorial University (Karen Loving) have obtained for me many
books and articles to which I would not otherwise have had
access.

My friends and family also have given me support, moral
and intellectual, physical and financial, enabling me to perse-
vere in this task. My colleagues at Lincoln Memorial University, especially my chair, Dan DeBord, and my buddies David
Sprague and Kay Davis, have offered me encouragement in
my scholarly efforts. My friend Whitney Stegall has assisted
me financially. Wera Howard and Nancy Rupprecht trans-
lated an article for me. Ginny Vesper obtained books. Bill
Geissler and Diti Geissler lent me a computer, and my brother
Arthur later built one for me, without which this book would
never have been completed. Many friends, such as John
Juricek, Linda Magee, Bascom Williamson and Mitsue
Williamson, and the Geisslers, have listened patiently while I
have expounded my ideas. My father-in-law, Paul Ferris, read
through rough drafts and offered sound editorial advice, as
did my husband, Norman, who also bought me books, ran
errands, obtained articles, tended children, dogs, cats, and
plants, cooked dinner, and hardly complained. My children
have humored me. My mother has been proud of me. This
work is the result of the contributions of many.

With gratitude

   to NORMAN,
whose love and support
have made this work possible,
and
   to my MOTHER,
who taught me to love books.

Prologue

Richard Ellmann's biography and critical writings on James Joyce, and his editing of the Joyce correspondence, form the foundation on which subsequent Joyceans, especially those of us who studied with him, have built. I am very grateful to Dr. Ellmann for the work to which he devoted so many years of his life. By gathering, preserving, and publishing so much information for his monumental study, *James Joyce*, he performed an invaluable service to future generations of Joyce scholars. However, just as a titanic writer can dominate an era and become a force from whom those who follow must seek to liberate themselves, so too can a powerful scholar cast an excessive influence over a field of studies. Ellmann's biography of Joyce, as Melvin J. Friedman recently observed, has been repeatedly referred to as "definitive" (*Reviewing Classics of Joyce Criticism* 133). This work has so dominated the field of Joyce studies that when we refer to Joyce, we refer to Ellmann's Joyce; there is no other. And we no longer write biographical criticism, because after Ellmann, what more is there to say?

In recent years, however, critics have begun to question the accuracy of Ellmann's portrayal. Articles by Phillip F. Herring, Ira B. Nadel, Joseph Kelly, and Morton Levitt have challenged the "definitive" status of the biography, suggesting that Ellmann relied too much upon speculation unsupported by factual evidence, that he inadequately portrayed the complexity of Joyce's personality, that he depended too heavily upon Joyce's brother Stanislaus as a source, and that he was a "total failure" as a critic because he distorted Joyce's art by making the works secondary to the life.[1] The consensus among Joyceans now seems to be that the Ellmann bi-

ography is an unreliable guide to Joyce's works, and that
"our understanding of Joyce the man still remains incomplete" (Nadel, "The Incomplete Joyce" 100). As more primary materials, including Ellmann's own personal papers, become available to scholars, it is inevitable that we reexamine and reevaluate existing portraits of the artist in the light of new information.

I too have found myself in disagreement with portions of the Ellmann biography. In two interrelated areas of Joyce's life, those of the writer's health and of his religious attitudes, I find Ellmann's work incomplete and misleading. In the first instance, Ellmann had in his possession significant materials, to which he never alluded, regarding Joyce's health. In the second, he chose to ignore the testimony of contemporary observers regarding Joyce's religious practices.

When Richard Ellmann began gathering information for his biography in the early 1950s, many of the people who had known Joyce were still alive. The decades following Joyce's death afforded rare opportunities for obtaining information, opportunities of which Ellmann took full advantage through the assiduous cultivation of Joyce's friends and family.[2] However, correspondence in the Ellmann papers at Tulsa and in the Jolas papers at Yale's Beinecke Library shows that the very relationships with Joyce's friends and family, built upon trust, which enabled Ellmann to gain access to primary materials also inhibited his making full use of them. Had he disclosed all that he learned about Joyce's life, not only would he have violated the confidence which he had worked so hard to gain, but he would also have hurt or angered a large number of people. Furthermore, the extent to which he was allowed to use materials might have been curtailed. Indeed, it was somewhat limited even so. For example, Harriet Shaw Weaver, Joyce's benefactress, gave Ellmann access to her letters from Joyce and from Paul Leon, except those about Lucia which she had destroyed, but she maintained tight control over what

might be quoted (Tulsa). Likewise, Joyce's friend Maria
Jolas made available to Ellmann a trunk of letters which
had been entrusted to her care before the family's departure for Zurich, but she swore the scholar to secrecy about
the existence of the materials, and she determined what and
how much he might use (Jolas Collection, Beinecke).[3] After
the segment of the biography covering the Paris years was
completed, Ellmann asked Maria to read it and make suggestions for changes. As the book was going to press, Maria
wanted to ask Joyce's son, Giorgio, for permission to use
correspondence between his parents, but Ellmann begged
her not to write to Giorgio, fearing the son would become
"censorious," explaining: "I made the changes you suggested
in the book, including the removal of passages that were
too blunt, and in general tried to heighten what was always
my intention, to bring the reader to sympathy with Joyce,
his life and his work, while not sacrificing honesty or objec-
tivity" (25 Feb. 1959, Jolas Collection, Beinecke). As Ellmann
said to Mrs. Jolas elsewhere, in a different context, trying
to gain access to primary materials was "all tightrope walking" (16 Dec. 1954, Beinecke). Certainly the business of
gathering information while avoiding censorship was a delicate balancing act.

Further evidence that Ellmann's relationships with
Joyce's friends and family affected what he published is to
be found in his correspondence with Joyce's grandson,
Stephen. On 17 December 1959, after the appearance of
Ellmann's biography, Stephen complained of his family's
intimate life being laid bare to the world. Ellmann wrote to
him: "I hope you will not think I have written my book
wholly without reserve. Your great-aunt May Monaghan
. . . wrote me . . . that she could see it was composed in
entire friendship for her family. I should like to think that
you would feel the same is true" (Richard Ellmann Collection, Tulsa). After the second edition of the biography appeared, Stephen again objected, this time to the publishing
of the autopsy report on his grandfather. On 17 February

1983, Ellmann replied: "The post mortem report has the effect of scotching rumors about the history of Joyce's ulcers and about other possible causes of death" (Tulsa). Hence it is no wonder that working under the close scrutiny of Joyce's family and friends, the biographer omitted telling all that he learned about Joyce's health when he interviewed Joyce's many physicians.

In 1955, at Ellmann's behest, his colleague at Northwestern University Robert Mayo called upon Dr. Arthur Collinson (then living in Boston), who had been one of Joyce's ophthalmologists in Paris, the younger partner of Dr. Borsch, who performed surgery on Joyce's eyes. Collinson told Mayo that syphilis was the "suspected" cause of Joyce's eye problems, a statement that later, perhaps remembering medical ethics regarding doctor-patient confidentiality, he tempered in a follow-up interview. Dr. Pierre Merigot de Treigny wrote to Ellmann, "Joyce wore very dark goggles and suffered of rheumatical iritis." Dr. Edward Hartmann explained to him that "Gonorrhea gives rheumatic iritis" (Tulsa). In 1930, Joyce himself had confided to Harriet Shaw Weaver: "a young French ophthalmologist, Dr. Hartmann, . . . said the only possible solution of the case was that my eye trouble proceeded from congenital syphilis" (*Selected Ltrs.* 348). A fourth doctor, Pierre V. Morax, wrote to Ellmann (my translation from French): "I do not think that very precise information on the ocular illness from which M. James Joyce suffered would be very useful to you. Furthermore, in principle, professional secrecy forbids revealing it to you" (Tulsa).[4] These statements from Joyce's physicians strongly suggest that his eye afflictions stemmed from venereal infection, yet nowhere does Ellmann mention even the possibility of such a connection, and nowhere does the word *syphilis* appear in his writings. He tells us only that in 1904, Joyce contracted "a minor ailment . . . during a visit to Nighttown," and that his friend, medical student Oliver St. John Gogarty, referred him to a physician for treatment (*JJ* 150).

Thus, during the five decades that have passed since Joyce's death, there has remained a great untold segment of Joyce's life that none of his biographers has explored. Only one, Stan Gebler Davies, mentions syphilis, and then only in the appendix of a biography written without footnotes. Davies attributes Joyce's eye ailments to the artist's father having acquired syphilis in his youth, an issue that I will address later.

The question of whether Joyce suffered from syphilis is not a new one. It has been repeatedly raised and denied by a Dublin physician, Dr. J.B. Lyons, who has written two books and several articles on the subject. In Ellmann's personal notebook at the University of Tulsa is an entry, "the Joyces were connected with Dr. Lyons . . . .He had Cork connections." Joyce's father was from Cork, and his mother's aunt was a Mrs. Lyons. The typescript of a letter from Joyce to Stanislaus (dated 21 September 1926, also at Tulsa) reports, "James Lyons flew over to see me in Ostende," indicating that Joyce's family ties to his Lyons relatives remained unbroken. In his latest work on Joyce, Dr. Lyons has written glowingly that Joyce's "love of family shines" in his poetry (*What Did I Die Of* 215). Furthermore, when Dr. Lyons first raised the issue of the cause of Joyce's eye ailments and eliminated syphilis from the possible causes, to my knowledge no one had yet suggested, at least not in writing, that Joyce might have suffered from syphilis. Perhaps rumors needed to be scotched.

With regard to Joyce's eye problems, Dr. Lyons has written:

> Syphilis was responsible for fifty per cent of cases of acute primary iritis in the first quarter of the present century but can be confidently excluded [as the cause of Joyce's iritis]: Syphilitic iritis usually occurs in the secondary stage of syphilis when other diagnostic signs abound; the Wasserman reaction (positive in syphilis) would have been a routine test in any eye clinic; pain tends to be slight and after two to eight weeks the iritis subsides and does not recur . . . .There

is nothing to suggest that Joyce had syphilis, but from the evidence of Gogarty's letters . . . it appears that he acquired gonorrhea, another cause of uveitis, in Dublin. (*James Joyce and Medicine* 204)

The results of my research on this topic in textbooks of ophthalmology do not support Dr. Lyons's confident assertions. The opinions of experts contradict the basis of Dr. Lyons's exclusion of syphilis as the cause of Joyce's eye problems, as well as his assertions that the symptoms of syphilitic iritis are slight and that the Wassermann reaction would necessarily be positive.[5] So to his injunction to "Thrust Syphilis down to Hell," at least one reader refuses to comply. In his book by this title, Dr. Lyons quotes the same letter to Harriet Weaver that I quoted earlier (*Selected Letters* 348) to prove that Joyce did *not* have the disease. Let us examine this letter more closely:

> a young French ophthalmologist, Dr. Hartmann, . . . said the only possible solution of the case was that my eye trouble proceeded from congenital syphilis, which being curable, he said the proper thing for me was to undergo a cure of I have forgotten what [at that time the cure would be arsenic]. I told this to Dr. Collinson and he dissuaded me strongly from undergoing it [the treatment]. He said that at the very beginning Dr. Borsch and he had discussed the possibility and that Borsch had excluded it [the treatment] categorically on account of the nature of the attacks, the way in which they were cured and the general reactions of the eye. . . . he had known cases in which the use of the drug in question had had a bad effect on the optic nerve. So that ended that for me.

As I interpret this passage, the possibility that Borsch excluded was the treatment, not the diagnosis, as Dr. Lyons suggests. (The question is one of pronoun reference.) The arsenical treatments used for syphilis often caused a Herxheimer reaction, a temporary exacerbation of symptoms which, in eyes as delicate as Joyce's, could have had disastrous consequences. Medical textbooks repeatedly cautioned physicians to beware, when dealing with cases of advanced syphilis, the danger of treating the disease at the expense of the patient. Readers can weigh Lyons's explanation, that Reiter's syndrome caused Joyce's eye problems, against the evidence that I will present, that they resulted from venereal disease, and decide for themselves which case is more plausible.

Other physicians also have written about Joyce's medical problems. Two articles of particular importance, co-authored by an American physician Dr. Burton A. Waisbren, appeared in 1974 and 1980 in the *Archives of Internal Medicine*. Both articles traced the theme of syphilis in writings of Joyce, the first in "The Sisters," the second in *Ulysses*. The authors do not imply that Joyce himself suffered from syphilis, only that he was writing about it. However, I have been told by scholars that Florence Walzl, who co-authored the article on "The Sisters," and whose husband was a physician, years ago, on more than one occasion, went before the International James Joyce Foundation and tried, without success, to persuade that body that Joyce had been infected.

My own interest in this subject began over a decade ago, while tracing the Wandering Jew theme in *Ulysses* for a graduate seminar paper at Emory University, before I knew that the idea of Joyce's having syphilis had ever occurred to anyone else. What I shall present in this work is the evidence, medical, biographical, and literary, which I have found linking the theme of guilt, which permeates Joyce's writings, to venereal disease, and showing that, in all probability, Joyce was infected with syphilis.

Not only is the art of biography a selective process, it is also a subjective one. The biographer colors his interpretation of facts according to his own temperament, values, and experience. This is not to say that biography is untruthful, only that as Leon Edel has pointed out, "there is no such thing as a completely 'objective' biography. . . .The biographer cannot remove himself from the story" (58). Ellmann's Joyce is a reflection of Ellmann. He is not the Joyce that I see. Ellmann was of Jewish background and was, I imagine, an enlightened humanist, whereas I, like Joyce, am a renegade Catholic. Undoubtedly my portrait of Joyce will also reflect something of my own cultural background. Where Ellmann saw Joyce's break with Christianity as total and final, I believe that no matter how completely a person separates himself from his Catholic origins, the world view, the sense of the sacredness of life, the moral values and the fears that a child acquires as part of his early religious training are likely to remain with the adult throughout his life. Catholic guilt is not easily escaped; nor is the Catholic impulse to confess. Hence I disagree with the assertion that Joyce became what Ellmann called a "secular artist" who used religious imagery simply as a metaphor for his art (*JJ* 66). Instead, I see his art as a means (to borrow a phrase from T.S. Eliot) of projecting and ordering the complex emotional material of his life, as a means of purging himself of the guilt that ensued from violating taboos imposed by the religion of his childhood. Joyce's brother Stanislaus recognized that emotional needs prompted Jim's writing: "I think he wrote to make things clear to himself . . . .my brother used patterns in his later work because he found a pattern even in the disorder of his own life; being an artist and not a philosopher . . . he made this personal experience the informing spirit of his later work" (*MBK* 54, 225). An undated letter from Joyce to his daughter Lucia (c. 1935) corroborates this notion: "I am slow O Yes 8 years to write a book and 18 for its successor. But I will understand in the end" (*Ltrs.* I: 377). The desire to impose the order of art over the chaos of experience is one impulse that lies behind the writing of autobiographical and confessional literature.[6] I will argue (*pace* Mort Levitt) that Joyce's later works are both autobiographical and confessional in nature.

Joyce's writings are filled with religious imagery which points to the theme of guilt. Biblical allusions and references to the legend of the Wandering Jew embedded in *Ulysses* all point, as I will show, to the ideas of sin and retribution. These allusions seem to me to have at least equal importance with the Homeric references about which so much has been written. If Homer provided the lighter warp, the humor, for the fabric of Joyce's works, then the Bible and Christian lore provided the darker woof, the tragedy. For these serious themes, however, Joyce drew up no schema. Instead he encouraged Stuart Gilbert to write a book explaining *Ulysses* solely in terms of its Homeric references. Gilbert's interpretations of Joyce's works were clearly biased: "*Work in Progress* like *Ulysses* is a richly comic work; nothing is here of highbrow gravity and the note of tragedy is never heard" (Gilbert Collection, birthday speech delivered on Feb. 2, 1935, University of Texas). In my opinion, Joyce's emphasis of his use of Homer in *Ulysses* served to obscure his more serious themes.

The works of complex modern authors such as Joyce, who filled their writings with their own private symbolism, frequently seem difficult to comprehend upon first reading, especially if read without guidance. And perhaps the greatest conundrum of all modern literature is *Finnegans Wake*. Scholars who have spent a lifetime working on this text do not claim entirely to understand it. Despite decades of effort in tracing literary and historical allusions, we still do not grasp the overall meaning of this gigantic word puzzle. For the reading of Joyce's works, so dense with personal symbols, the more we learn about the man, the more the works will become elucidated, because the literary work and the creative mind reflect each other. In the words of Ernst Cassirer, "In language, in religion, in art, in science, man can do no more than build up his own universe—a symbolic universe that enables him to understand and interpret, to articulate and organize, to synthesize and universalize *his human experience*" (emphasis added) (Quoted in Olney 6). Much of our understanding of an author's works is based upon our knowledge of his/her experiences and thoughts,

not entirely, as Vicki Mahaffey suggests, upon our construct
of the author in our own self-image (28). Leon Edel noted
nearly three decades ago: "Critical judgment . . . must ac-
cord with all that we know of a writer's temperament and
the literary ambiance in which it functioned . . . .Biographi-
cal and historical evidence are the foundations upon which
criticism can truly function" (68). Edel's description of the
relationship of the life of the author to his creative work
applies very well to Joyce:

> The . . . work is in a certain sense a kind of supreme biog-
> raphy of the artist and a projection of his *persona* in many
> disguises . . . .creative writers do their work out of pro-
> found inner dictates and in response to the ways in which
> their emotions and their views of the world have been
> formed. With all the world to choose from, they invariably
> select subjects closest to their inner feelings; and when they
> choose subjects seemingly alien to them, they invariably alter
> them to correspond to their personal condition, even though
> what emerges may seem, to the uninitiated, remote and
> unrelated . . . .In this sense it might be said that writers—
> and writers of fiction in particular—are always engaged in
> creating parables about themselves. (62-63)

One perceptive reader of Joyce's works, Thornton Wilder,
observed many years ago,

> James Joyce was hunting for a style that would reveal the
> extent to which every individual is sole and unique and
> also archetypical . . . .he had to draw on the human being
> whom he knew best: himself. So the book [*Finnegans Wake*]
> likewise is a confession, and it is confession at a very deep
> and agonizing level. It is a wonderful experience to unbur-
> den the heart in confession, but it is a very difficult thing to
> do. The subject longs to tell his charged secret and longs
> not to tell it. So the complications are partly one step for-
> ward and two steps back and two steps forward and four
> steps back. *Finnegans Wake* is, in spite of all we know of its
> comic force and its lyric beauty, an agonized journey into
> the private life of James Joyce. (11-12)

For over three decades, however, Joyce's critics, even while recognizing the autobiographical nature of his writings, have been operating with an incomplete biographical construct, and this lack of information about some of the most sensitive aspects of Joyce's life has affected the kinds of interpretations written. For instance, Zack Bowen's critical study of *Ulysses*, which places Joyce within the comic tradition of Western literature, interprets the novel as light-hearted comedy (Ulysses *as a Comic Novel*), and Mark Shechner interprets Joyce's preoccupation with syphilis as "an Irish joke" (127). These readings are consistent with Ellmann's portrayal of "Sunny Jim" who liberated himself from the nets of nationality, language, and religion. My reading of Joyce, by contrast, will seem gloomy, tracing the recurrent themes of sin, guilt, and repentance that echo throughout *A Portrait of the Artist as a Young Man, Ulysses,* and *Finnegans Wake,* for my view of Joyce is a darker one; I see a man who never escaped the nets of his past, particularly the nets of religion and disease. I agree with Joseph Campbell's assessment of the mythic imagery in *Ulysses,* that Joyce identifies with the "soul of darkness" rather than with the "soul of light," with the sinners Esau and Cain rather than with Jacob and Abel (*The Masks of God: Creative Mythology* 661). Certainly this is not to deny the comic elements in Joyce's works, nor to deny that those works belong within the European comic tradition. But I would place Joyce also within the tradition of Irish writers—Synge, O'Casey, Beckett—whose mode is tragicomic. Their humor is dark, bitter, and satiric. And I will attempt to show the circumstances of Joyce's life that transformed young "Sunny Jim" into a "Man of Sorrows."

Joyce was not candid about his life, nor about his artistic purposes, nor about his emotional ties to Ireland and to Catholicism. He deliberately tried to censor the facts of his life for Herbert Gorman's biography, and on the question of religion, Ellmann repeated the erroneous assumptions of Joyce's first biographer. Only the recent biography by

Morris Beja, *James Joyce, A Literary Biography*, has somewhat corrected these misconceptions: "for the rest of his life Joyce remained profoundly influenced by the dogma, ritual, and processes of reasoning he had learned within the Church: the least that could be said of him is what Mulligan says of Stephen: 'you have the cursed jesuit strain in you, only it's injected the wrong way'" (9).

Both of Joyce's earlier biographers represent the artist's youthful rejection of Roman Catholicism as an act of will by which a free-spirited young man liberated himself from the shackles of Irish parochialism, essentially the same story that Joyce told about Stephen in *Portrait of the Artist*. Gorman writes: "The religious faith he had professed (and, for a period, violently) as a boy was dying down in his spirit as a ruddy coal dims in a neglected fire" (56). And Ellmann states: "Christianity had subtly evolved in his mind from a religion into a system of metaphors, which as metaphors could claim his fierce allegiance . . . .He was no longer a Christian himself; but he converted the temple to new uses instead of trying to knock it down, regarding it as a superior kind of human folly and one which, interpreted by a secular artist, contained obscured bits of truth" (*JJ* 66).

To assume that Joyce was capable of sloughing off sixteen years of Jesuit indoctrination like an old coat, or of cutting it into pieces to incorporate into his new garment, is similar to assuming that when he departed from Ireland for the last time, he severed the bonds to his native land. His denunciations of the Church, like the statement "I loathe Ireland and the Irish," are hardly to be taken as an accurate and permanent indication of the state of his feelings, which were as ambivalent as they were strong (*Ltrs.* II: 255).

During the years after Joyce departed from Ireland, there is ample evidence that he retained emotional ties to his Catholic past, even if he never did return to the embrace of Mother Church. Alessandro Francini Bruni, one of Joyce's closest friends in Pola and Trieste, recalls those days:

In his house there is no religious practice, but . . . there is much talk of Christ and religion and much singing of liturgical chants. I can go even further. You had better not look for Joyce during the week before Easter because he is not available to anyone. On the morning of Palm Sunday, then during the four days that follow Wednesday of Holy Week, and especially during all the hours of those great symbolic rituals at the early morning service, Joyce is at church, . . . sitting in full view and close to the officiants so that he won't miss a single syllable of what is said, following the liturgy attentively in his book of the Holy Week services, and often joining in the singing of the choir. (Potts 35)

Stanislaus's unpublished Trieste diary confirms this account. The diary further indicates that as late as August of 1908, Joyce had stated that his religious faith was not completely extinguished: "Jim said this evening that he believed that in his heart everyman was religious. He spoke from his knowledge of himself. I asked him did he mean that every man had in his heart some faith in a Deity, by which he could be influenced. He said, 'Yes'" (Ellmann Collection, Tulsa).

Joyce's lifelong churchgoing seems to indicate that despite his rejection of the authority of the Roman church, his personal religious faith and practices persisted. In 1902 from Paris he had written to his mother to ask Stannie to "Send Holy Week Book in time for Tenebrae on Wednesday" (*Ltrs.* II: 40). During his sojourn in Rome in 1906-7, not only did he visit Roman Catholic cathedrals, but also, as his correspondence with Stanislaus attests, he repeatedly attended services. On one occasion he wrote enthusiastically, "They are celebrating this week in Sylvester's Church the union of the rites. Every morning a different rite. I should *love* to go" (*Ltrs.* II: 206). Joyce's sister Eileen remembered that in Trieste, "He used to go to the Greek Orthodox church because he said he liked the ceremonies better there. But in Holy Week he always went to the Catholic Church. He said that Catholics were the only people who

knew how to keep Holy Week" (Curtayne 45). When Eileen
was asked, "It must have been after Trieste, then, that he
gave up the practice of religion?" she replied, "Did he ever
give it up? He took Nora's sister to Mass in England. Years
and years after, when I stayed with them in Paris, he went
to Mass too, but always by himself." Jacques Mercanton,
too, who knew Joyce in Paris, recalls that as late as 1938 the
author was still attending church on Good Friday and Holy
Saturday, services of penitence (Potts 214-15). *Finnegans
Wake* refers to "Jimmy the chapelgoer" (587.35). Thus we
have testimony from diverse sources that Joyce maintained
a lifelong practice of observing the Christian week of penitence, a season which held deep significance for him.

What I invite my readers to do is to suspend Ellmann's
construct of Joyce as a secular humanist and to consider my
very different representation of the artist as a guilt-ridden,
diseased, deracinated Catholic who repented his sins, and
whose works form an allegory of his life, an account of his
emotional and spiritual journey.

1
The Creative Daemon

For the creative artist, the act of writing frequently is the result of an inner compulsion, the fulfillment of a need. Sometimes the creative impulse stems from a desire to communicate to others whatever special insights the author has gained through the process of living, to share one's world view. Writing can also be a means of communicating with the hidden, unconscious part of oneself, or it can be an act of catharsis. As we have noted, for Joyce, writing was a way of ordering experience to try to make sense out of life. It was also an act of purgation. In him, the creative urge seems to be rooted in sin and guilt; throughout his writings we find these motifs resonating.

In an essay he wrote on Oscar Wilde in 1909, five years after he and Nora departed for the continent, Joyce emphasizes the importance of sin in the art and life of that writer, in words that echo some of his own themes:

> Here we touch the pulse of Wilde's art—sin. He deceived himself into believing that he was the bearer of good news of neo-paganism to an enslaved people. His own distinctive qualities, the qualities, perhaps, of his race—keenness, generosity, and a sexless intellect—he placed at the service of a theory of beauty which, according to him, was to bring back the Golden Age and the joy of the world's youth. But if some truth adheres to his subjective interpretations of Aristotle, . . . at its very base is the truth inherent in the soul of Catholicism: that man cannot reach the divine heart except through that sense of separation and loss called sin. (*Critical Writings* 204-5)

We could attribute Joyce's preoccupation with sin to his religious upbringing, but to explain this concern solely in terms of his Roman Catholic background would be a case of oversimplification; certainly many other Irish Catholic write—Padraic Colum, Frank O'Connor, Patrick Kavanagh, Austin Clarke, to name only a few—have managed to escape the degree of obsession with sin and guilt that permeates Joyce's works. The trait seems a personal one with him, not to be dismissed as merely part of a cultural phenomenon. Many critics have commented upon the theme of guilt in Joyce's writings, as did Darcy O'Brien in *The Conscience of Joyce* in 1968, but heretofore scholars have not fully explored the source of this personal preoccupation.

In order to locate the mainsprings of Joyce's creativity, it is helpful to look beyond existing biographical constructs of the artist to his own words, where the patterns of his thought are to be found in the metaphors he used in reference to himself. Frequently what he says through indirection is more revealing than what is stated more bluntly. In his works, both published and unpublished, we find a number of recurrent images and figures of speech that he used to describe himself.

From earliest childhood, Joyce seems to have identified with Satan, the Arch-Sinner. At first, the feelings he attached to this self-image were not altogether negative. Early in his life especially, he enjoyed playing the bad boy. According to his brother Stanislaus, when he was a young child, Joyce directed the children of the family nursery in a dramatization of the fall of Adam and Eve, reserving for himself the role of serpent (*MBK* 27). Joyce's childhood playmate, Eileen Vance Harris, tells a similar story, that "Jimmie had his own way of punishing his small brothers and sisters when they displeased him. He had a red stocking cap and a little red wheelbarrow. The offending child was made to lie on the ground, the wheelbarrow was put over him, and Jimmie donned the red cap. Now he was the Devil and made sounds to indicate that the offender under the wheelbarrow was being burned in Hell" (Ellmann Collection, Tulsa).

As a young man, Joyce again assumed a diabolic role,

this time of a lofty Miltonic Satan, in a satiric broadside,
"The Holy Office," fired at his fellow writers just before he
left Ireland to reside permanently on the European continent:

> Where they have crouched and crawled and prayed
> I stand, the self-doomed, unafraid,
> Unfellowed, friendless and alone.
>
> (*Portable JJ* 659)

Stephen Dedalus strikes a similar pose when like Lucifer he declares: "*Non serviam*" (*Portrait* 239; *Ulysses* 15.4228).
References to Milton's Satan and to *Paradise Lost* also occur
in *Finnegans Wake* (Schork).

Toward the end of his life, when writing a children's
story for his grandson Stephen, a story about the devil and
a cat, Joyce once more identified himself with Satan in the
postscript appended to his letter: "The devil mostly speaks
a language of his own called Bellsybabble which he makes
up himself as he goes along but when he is very angry he
can speak quite bad French very well though some who have
heard him say he has a strong Dublin accent" (*Ltrs.* I: 388).

Joyce's early Satanic posturings were perhaps merely
the expression of an overactive imagination or of youthful
arrogance; however, the consistency of his use of diabolic
imagery in reference to himself suggests a deeply instilled
sense of his own sinfulness, a self-image that was to have a
profound effect on his life and art. Though with the passage of time, the proud, "self-doomed" Satan deteriorated
into a babbling old devil, he remained among the company
of the damned.

Perhaps one reason Joyce maintained this view of himself as sinner is that he identified with his scalawag father,
upon whose death he wrote to Harriet Shaw Weaver, "I was
very fond of him always, being a sinner myself, and even
liked his faults" (*Ltrs.* I: 312). He also liked and identified
with historical and literary sinners, filling his works with

mythic outcasts. The figure of Cain seems particularly to have captured his imagination. In 1928 he sent to an American composer in Paris, George Anthiel, a copy of Byron's drama *Cain*, suggesting that he use it as a libretto for an opera. The "Circe" episode of *Ulysses*, which he also wanted Anthiel to set to music, has Leopold Bloom branded with the letter C, the mark of Cain, and in *Finnegans Wake* Finn MacCool is told, "Just press this cold brand against your brow for a mow. Cainfully! The sinus the curse" (374.32). Many of the Biblical references in *Ulysses* are to great sinners: Stephen quotes not only Lucifer, but also Esau, King Ahab, and the Prodigal Son; Lynch is referred to as Judas; and Bloom is called the Antichrist and the Wandering Jew.

Frequently in private correspondence, Joyce's allusions to sin are made in jest, such as, "Writing in English is the most ingenious torture ever devised for sins committed in previous lives," and "Is not this adding a new horror to eternal punishment?" and "O dear me! What sins did I commit in my last incarnation to be in this hole?" (*Ltrs.* I: 120; III: 79; II: 88). In moments of dejection, however, his self-denigration knew no limits. To his benefactress, Harriet Shaw Weaver, he refers to "the dark side of my despicable character," and to his wife, he says, "Take away your children from me to save them from the curse of my presence. Let me sink back into the mire I came from . . . . It is wrong for you to live with a vile beast like me or to allow your children to be touched by my hands" (*Ltrs.* I: 167; II: 265).

In this last example is another recurrent image by which Joyce conveys the idea of his own sinfulness, the metaphor of physical filth to represent spiritual corruption. In "The Holy Office," he satirically describes the cathartic role of the poet by portraying himself in the function of a sewer:

> That they may drem their dreamy dreams
> I carry off their filthy streams.
> For I can do those things for them
> Through which I lost my diadem,

Those things for which Grandmother Church
Left me severely in the lurch.
Thus I relieve their timid arses,
Perform my office of Katharsis.

(Portable JJ 658)

References to physical filth continue in his depiction of literary characters. In *Portrait of the Artist as a Young Man,* when
young Stephen Dedalus is pushed into an open sewage ditch
by an older boy and consequently becomes very ill, the action prefigures Stephen's later fall in a Dublin brothel, into
the "foul swamp of sin" (114). The first fall, which results
in disease, is probably not biographical, for Joyce's brother
Stanislaus remembers that Jim was in perfect health during
his years at Clongowes Wood College (*MBK* 41); the second, as Stanislaus's diaries show, undoubtedly is. In *Ulysses,*
Leopold Bloom is described as "that vigilant wanderer,
soiled by the dust of travel and combat and stained by the
mire of an indelible dishonour," and Stephen is called "the
unclean bard" because, like Joyce, he refuses to bathe
(14.1217-18; 1.475). In *Finnegans Wake* the washerwomen
at the Ford refer to HCE as "duddurty devil" (196.15), and
Justius tells Shem, "You will need all the elements in the
river to clean you over it all and a fortifine popespriestpower
bull of attender to booth" (188.5). Stanislaus recalls Joyce's
hygiene as a university student: "During a parlour game
called 'Confession,' when asked what was his pet aversion,
he answered promptly 'Soap and water,' and I believe it
was the truth" (*MBK* 123). One possible explanation of this
behavior is given by psychologist Theodor Reik: "Analytic
observation shows . . . that neglect of cleanliness, dirt itself,
becomes an unconscious sign of a feeling of guilt" (345). In
Ulysses, Stephen too makes a correlation between dirt and
guilt: "They wash and tub and scrub. Agenbite of inwit.
Conscience. Yet here's a spot" (1.481-82).

Yet Joyce had not always been a hydrophobe. J.F. Byrne,
who had known him from boyhood, recalls: "Joyce was . . .

a good swimmer, and during the summer months in the late 90's he frequented the Bull Wall, at the southwest side, where he swam or sat sunning on the rocks, attired, like all the boys and young men at that place, in nothing at all" (176). By his later years, Joyce had acquired an avid dislike for public bathing. Jacques Mercanton recalls that he watched bathers "with horror" and "with his usual dread" (Potts 216, 236). Writing to his son Giorgio, who was vacationing at a seaside resort, Joyce explained his refusal to swim: "I should take a bath too but I am too proud. Or perhaps I have too much respect for the water" (*Ltrs*. III: 361). Joyce's words imply that his own dirt would contaminate the ocean.

In Christian cultures, sexual sins are traditionally associated with the notion of filth, perhaps because since the late fifteenth century, promiscuity has been known to lead to disease. In his writing Joyce repeatedly juxtaposes images of dirt and sexually transmitted infections. In *Giacomo Joyce*, an autobiographical vignette written in Trieste c. 1914, we see the image of "the cesspool of the court of slobbering James" with "the pox-fouled wenches and young wives that, gaily yielding to their ravishers, clip and clip again" (9). In the "Epilogue to Ibsen's *Ghosts*" that Joyce wrote in 1932, the ghost of Captain Alving (who during his lifetime had infected his wife and child with syphilis) compares himself to a "lewd knight in dirty linen" (Yale). Stephen's guilt and repentance for his sins in *Portrait of the Artist* are expressed in terms of mire, excrement, corruption, foulness, infection. His confession is described thus: "His sins trickled from his lips, one by one, trickled in shameful drops from his soul festering and oozing like a sore, a squalid stream of vice. The last sins oozed forth, sluggish, filthy" (144). The old priest warns Stephen in the confessional of the physical as well as the spiritual consequences of his actions: "You are very young, my child, he said, and let me implore of you to give up that sin. It is a terrible sin. It kills the body and it kills the soul" (144-45). The priest is clearly warning the boy against the dangers of venereal infection. As Allan M. Brandt has noted, victims of venereal disease think of themselves as filthy, or contaminated, or poisoned. He quotes one sufferer of herpes as saying, "You never think you're clean enough" (181). Thus the images of filth which Joyce chose to describe his characters and himself convey associations both psychological and physical. They are an especially good example of the manner in which he uses imagery and allusion to create allegorical representations of his own life. As we shall see, Stephen Dedalus's fall into the sewage ditch and the life-threatening illness that resulted are symbolic of Joyce's own fall into the "foul swamp of sin" in brothels and of his consequent illness.

In Roman Catholicism, sin is washed away by the waters of Baptism, by the Blood of the Lamb, by the priest washing his hands before the consecration of the host, by annointing the senses of the dying person with holy oil, and by the sacrament of Confession. In *Finnegans Wake*, Joyce associates the ideas of washing and the need for confession. Justius suggests that unclean Shem say a "homely little confiteor about things" (188.4), and the old washerwomen, trying to scour the dirt and stain of sin out of the laundry of HCE and ALP, paraphrase the opening words of the penitent in the confessional, "Baptise me, father, for she has sinned!" (204.36) As Father William T. Noon has noted, Joyce ends *Finnegans Wake* with a pun on the words "wash-up" and "worship" (130).

The same reasoning which lies behind Joyce's explanation to his son, that neither pride alone, nor aversion to water, but a deep sense of his own uncleanness kept him from bathing, lies behind Stephen Dedalus's refusal to worship:

> Devotion had gone by the board. What did it avail to pray when he knew that his soul lusted after its own destruction? A certain pride, a certain awe, withheld him from offering to God even one prayer at night though he knew it was in God's power to take away his life while he slept and

hurl his soul hellward ere he could beg for mercy. His pride in his own sin, his loveless awe of God, told him that his offence was too grievous to be atoned for in whole or in part by a false homage to the Allseeing and Allknowing. (*Portrait* 103-4)

The refusal to worship, like the refusal to wash-up, comes from a sense of unworthiness. Perhaps Joyce, like Stephen, became estranged from God not because of lack of faith, but from a sense that his offence against God was "too grievous to be atoned for."

According to his own words, his rebellion against the church was not intellectual but emotional. He explained to his fiancée, Nora Barnacle: "Six years ago I left the Catholic Church, hating it most fervently. I found it impossible for me to remain in it on account of the impulses of my nature . . . . I cannot enter the social order except as a vagabond" (*Ltrs.* II: 48). Many years later, in discussing his religious crisis with the writer Padraic Colum, Joyce said, "Mind you, it was not a question of belief. It was a question of celibacy. I knew I could not live the life of a celibate" (*Our Friend James Joyce* 205-6).

For Joyce, as for Stephen, the issues of religion and sex polarized themselves in his mind. Faced with a choice between sanctity or sin, celibacy or excess, he chose the role of the sinner. At first the decision gave him a wonderful sense of exhilaration, of liberation from taboos. Now he could permit his appetites, never well-controlled, free rein. This euphoria was short-lived, however, both for Joyce and for Stephen.[1] The exultant Stephen at the close of *Portrait of the Artist as a Young Man* is quite a different character from the dejected Stephen at the opening of *Ulysses*. Like his creator, Stephen had suffered the loss of his mother in the intervening time. This catastrophic event had plunged the author into the worst period of debauchery of his whole life, the period of his association with Oliver St. John Gogarty, the period he depicts in Stephen's life in *Ulysses*. According to the Dublin diary of Stanislaus, this is when Joyce began drinking heavily, and Stannie blamed Gogarty for encouraging him. Whoring had begun earlier, according to Stanislaus's Trieste Dairy, as early as age fourteen; Gogarty could not be held responsible there (Trieste Diary, Tulsa). It was also during this time, in the spring of 1904, that Joyce was first treated for venereal disease.

If Stephen is indeed the alter ego of young Joyce, then illness might also contribute to his dejection. This would account for much of his resentment toward Malachi Mulligan, whose taunts in the opening chapter of *Ulysses* suggest that Stephen suffers from g.p.i. General paralysis of the insane is a layman's term for paresis, a form of neurosyphilis which leads to insanity.[2]

As most readers of *Ulysses* learn early in their study of the novel, the character Buck Mulligan is modeled on Oliver St. John Gogarty, a Dublin medical student who had been a close friend of Joyce's. A rupture had occurred in their friendship which embittered Joyce and caused him to lampoon Gogarty as the tactless, insensitive, irreverent joker Mulligan. Exactly what happened to cause Joyce to become so hostile as to create this devastating likeness, one which Gogarty's acquaintances easily recognized, is a question that has never been answered satisfactorily.

The two young men had been constant companions during the time that they were both in Dublin during the years 1902 to 1904. Besides sharing an interest in whoring and drink, they were both avid students of literature with ambitions to become writers. As might be expected between two young men of great intelligence and wit, an intense rivalry arose between them to see who could outdo the other. For these two, the competition was in the field of writing poems and bawdy limericks (Sheehy 28).

Joyce's brother Stanislaus disliked Gogarty, saying that he told Jim's business to everyone (*Diary* 26), and Richard

Ellmann adopted a similarly negative attitude toward Gogarty, referring to his "blend of savage wit and ambition" and calling him "addicted to obscenity and blasphemy" (*JJ* 173, 117).[3] James Carens, Gogarty's biographer, accuses Ellmann of failing to distinguish between Buck Mulligan, whom Stephen Dedalus characterized as "brutal and cruel," and the real person, Oliver Gogarty, who was neither. Carens quotes Irish writer Sean O'Faolain's description of Gogarty as "a kind and sensitive man, full of verve and zest . . . .His essential nature, which nobody could ever possibly gather from *Ulysses*, was his nature as a poet" (20). There are other testimonies as well, from people who knew Gogarty during his lifetime, as to his generous nature. Even Stanislaus tells of several instances in which Gogarty, who was the son of a wealthy widow, lent money to Jim, and not only money, but also his best clothes when Joyce participated in a singing competition.

The one quality of Gogarty's upon which everyone who writes about him seems agreed is his wit. His ribald sense of humor was reflected in scores of poems and limericks that he wrote and circulated, poems that have been published only in fragments, but which some readers thought to be of greater artistry than the serious poetry of which he eventually published several volumes. Joyce remembered many of these bawdy, irreverent poems and quoted or alluded to them in *Ulysses*: "The Song of the Cheerful (but slightly sarcastic) Jesus," "Sindbad," the "Medical Student's Song," and "Rosalie the Coalquay Whore" (Carens 25). Some of these poems are known to be addressed to Joyce, such as the limerick quoted by Stanislaus:

> There is a young fellow named Joyce,
> Who possesses a sweet tenor voice.
> He goes down to the kips
> With a psalm on his lips
> And biddeth the harlots rejoice.
> (*MBK* 160-61)

One mutual acquaintance of Gogarty and Joyce, Constantine Curran, claims that Gogarty's characterizing Joyce in verse was not done maliciously, that he did the same to all of his friends (75-76). But Padraic Colum describes Gogarty's wit in a less favorable light:

> He had a defect that prevented his being a companionable man—the gravest of defects, perhaps: he had no reserve in speaking about people, even those whom he had cause to admire, even those who were close to him. If they had some pitiful disability or shortcoming, he brought it right out. It was an incontinence of speech with Gogarty that was in itself a defect. One might think it was for the sake of making a witty point that he maligned others, and sometimes it was that. But, exposed to it for a while, one began to see that the trait was basic: Oliver Gogarty could not help but see some oddness, infirmity, or delinquency in a person talked about. The result was that people gave him license and kept a distance from him. (*Our Friend* 67)

These two tendencies of Gogarty, to write witty poems about his friends and to talk openly about their defects, will account, I believe, for the alienation of Joyce's friendship. In the Joyce collection of manuscripts at Cornell's Kroch Library are letters and poems written by Gogarty to Joyce, most of them dated 1904, the same year that Joyce left the Martello Tower, the same year that he eloped with Nora Barnacle for the continent. The contents of these letters are frequently obscene, which may account for the manner in which Richard Ellmann glossed over them in his biography. However, because of what they reveal about Joyce's life at that period, and about this significant literary relationship, they are of critical importance to Joyce scholars.

This is Ellmann's version of the episode to which the correspondence alludes: "On March 13, he [Joyce] was out all night, and not long after he had to write Gogarty, who was away at Oxford, to give him the name of a physician who would cure a minor ailment contracted during a visit to Nighttown" (*JJ* 150).

Actually, a letter from Gogarty, dated a month earlier on 13 February 1904, chides Joyce about the necessity for chastity and asks him to, "Let me hear about your dingus" (Joyce Collection, Cornell, #531).[4] It is followed by two letters of 10 March, one to Joyce and the other to Dr. Mick Walsh. To Joyce he wrote:

> Congratulations that our holy mother has judged you worthy of the stigmata . . . . If I would venture an opinion—you have got slight gleet from a *recurrence* of original sin. But you'll be all right. When next mounting be careful not to wish eternal blasting as *the process is intermittent.* Won't you write and tell me the news . . . . Don't let any laziness prevent you from presenting the letter as it may become incurable if neglected *or if you drink.* (Emphasis added.) (Cornell #533)

His letter to the doctor is as follows:

> My dear Mick:
> A friend of mine has been seeking employment as a water-clock and as he has not met with much success would be glad if he could re-convert his urethra to periodic and voluntary functions. I take the liberty of asking you to advise him from this note as I cannot introduce him myself,—being busy teaching the language to the natives here. Mr. Joyce is the name of the tissues surrounding the infected part if you will dam him you will delight me. He may have waited too long and got gleet. (Cornell #534)

For decades, scholars have assumed that the symptoms described here refer to gleet which accompanies gonorrhea (an assumption made by Dr. J.B. Lyons) and that the condition was temporary. An important fact to remember is that Gogarty calls the condition *recurrent,* and *intermittent.* These terms suggest the cyclic phases of syphilis. Furthermore, Samuel Beckett, who knew Joyce in Paris many years later, told Richard Ellmann that Joyce "wore two newspapers in his pants," a remark that bewildered Ellmann, but which seems to indicate that Joyce suffered from longterm incontinence, not from temporary gleet (Ellmann Collection). Both *Ulysses* and the *Wake* abound in references to waterclocks, waterclosets, and waterworks, inspired, I believe, by Gogarty's witty comparison of Joyce's condition to that of a waterclock.

The next letter is dated 3 May 1904 and is captioned, "The Bard Gogarty to the Wandering Aengus":

> My dear Joyce:
> may'st gain Eurydice from the infernal ones on your descent today! I hope you will keep clear of the "rout" that makes the hideous roar, in other words that the so long neglected ladies will not overcome you afterwards. Wire immediately the result is heard, and raise, on the victory falling to you, 5£ and come here for a week . . . . without faith we cannot be healed. Good luck old man: Give this "to Elwood Poxed."

What follows are two poems, a parody of Yeats's "The Pity of Love" and a fragment, both containing references to syphilis. Here is the first:

> In the house where whores are dwelling
> Unless it is wrapped in a glove
> A little Hunterian swelling
> Poxes the part that they love.

The "Hunterian swelling" to which Gogarty refers is a syphilitic chancre. The allusion is to the eighteenth-century English physician John Hunter, famous in medical annals because he inoculated himself with gonorrhea but contracted syphilis (or pox, as it was earlier called), of which he died, believing he had proved that the two diseases were the same. Actually, the two infections frequently are mixed and occur simultaneously. (This is another important fact to remember.)

A postscript on Gogarty's letter reads: "Thas a poem as yet in the head of the father, Chaos—to Elwood/the end

would be/[It] scalded when he pissed/And now he prays
to Mercury/Who was an atheist" (Cornell #536). The reference to mercury is significant. At this time mercury was
the prescribed treatment for syphilis, not for the so-called
"minor ailment" of gonorrhea. Furthermore, the belief then
held by doctors, that the imbibing of alcohol exacerbated
syphilitic infections, would account for Gogarty's admon-
ishing Joyce not to drink (contrary to Stanislaus's assumption that he encouraged Joyce to do so). It was not long
after this, on August 13 according to Stanislaus's Dublin
diary, that Joyce began to talk, "of the syphilitic contagion
in Europe . . . .The drift of his talk is that the contagion is
congenital and incurable and responsible for all manias,
and being so, that it is useless to try to avoid it" (51). Also,
according to J.F. Byrne, it was in "the early part of 1904"
that Joyce began to contemplate leaving Ireland (Tulsa).

Another letter, not dated, from Gogarty to Joyce during approximately the same period reads: "Has the second
consul fallen? Are the '_noble_ Kinsmen' undone? Well, the
canker has attacked Art and made it as dogmatic as emo-
tion" (Cornell #537). The image of the canker that destroys
the blossom is a metaphor that was to reappear years later
as the earwig in _Finnegans Wake._ It is also suggested by the
image of Leopold Bloom's "languid floating flower" at the
end of "Lotus Eaters."

On June ll Gogarty wrote to Joyce that he could not
send money, then asked, "How's Elwood?" (Cornell #538).
Their letters must have crossed, for on June 3 Joyce had
written Gogarty, "Elwood's nearly cured. I have a rendezvous with Annie Langton" (Harvard, Houghton Library).
John Elwood was another medical student who had frequently accompanied Joyce and Gogarty about Dublin. His
name is used by his companions in their correspondence as
a euphemism, I believe, for Joyce's diseased genitals. One
can only wonder what became of poor Annie Langton.

Among the letters from Gogarty is a poem, undated,
but of generally the same period, "To James Augustine

Joyce this work is dedicated as I wish to have before my work the holder of the highest of contemporary names and the hugest of contemporary tools." The poem, decorated with winged penises and entitled, "Song," begins thus:

> The First was Medical Dick
> The Second was Medical Davy
> The First had a Bloody Big Prick
> The Second had Buckets of Gravy
> to show—to show—to show what medicals are.

This is followed by three more stanzas, the import of which is that Medical Davy taunts his friend Medical Dick because he cannot perform sexually in spite of his enormous size, a condition which sounds like the result of a venereal infection. (Joyce too, we recall, was a medical student for a brief period of time.) Some years later, in 1907, Gogarty wrote a play for the Abbey Theatre entitled *Blight*, in which two characters named Medical Dick and Medical Davy discuss the ways by which a person can contract syphilis (*The Plays of Oliver Gogarty*). Joyce possessed a copy of *Blight* in his Trieste library, and, as we know, he used these medical characters both in *Ulysses* and in *Finnegans Wake*.

Blight is not the only work in which Gogarty made oblique reference to syphilis. In his "unpremeditated" biography, shortly after discussing his differences with Joyce, he wrote, "I do not wish to pose as a blameless observer of my friend Joyce . . . .After all, who am I to talk about sanity? Out of four of my friends, two committed suicide, one contracted syphilis, and the fourth was a schizophrene" (72). If he is counting Joyce among his friends, only the third or fourth descriptions could apply to him. It is unlikely that Gogarty would have said directly, in print, that Joyce was the friend who had contracted syphilis, but he does seem to be hinting at that possibility in this work which was published years after Joyce's death.

James Carens, who has written extensively on Gogarty,

finds Joyce's use of biographical material in his fictions as indicative of "a significant stratum of buried personal meanings and private allusions" ("Joyce and Gogarty" 37). My belief is that both Joyce and Gogarty buried personal messages in their writings as a means of communicating indirectly with each other after all direct communication had ceased. Joyce had a book by Gogarty on his desk at the time of his death.

Gogarty liked to exhibit his clever poems, which must have been a source of great embarrassment to Joyce. The one about the medical students was apparently sent directly to Joyce and may not have been seen by anyone else, but another of his masterpieces, the ballad of "Sindbad," subtitled "The Voyage of the Morbid Mariner," was circulated among their friends. Sindbad was a syphilitic sailor "Who by degrees/Passed from the primal Hunter's sore/To tertiaries" (fourteen stanzas of this poem, hand copied by an unidentified person, are to be found at the University of Texas, Austin). Gogarty sent word to Joyce after the latter had departed from Ireland, that "Sindbad" was in its 236th verse. Here are two of the stanzas that have been published:

> O what a wondrous paradox!
> A sailor who escaped the rocks
> Was wrecked by going down the docks
>   When safe ashore;
> And brought to light a hidden pox
>   And Hunter's sore
>   (Carens 26)

> Ah, did he, when he weighed his anchor,
> Weigh all the consequence of chancre?
> For if he did he would not hanker . . .
>   (U. O'Connor 122)

According to Carens, this poem is "an elaborate account of the adventures of a poxy sailor who has been pumped so full of Mercury that he is knocked unconscious by the rising and volatile liquid if he so much as stands too close to a source of heat" (*Surpassing Wit* 26). Finally Sindbad is thrown overboard and swallowed by a whale whose digestive system is upset by the mercury:

> Where that cetacean defecated
> A continent was concentrated
> From all the food evacuated
> Which was no mean land;
> And from its colour, when located,
> They called it Greenland.
>   (Carens, *Surpassing Wit* 150)

Joyce incorporates images from Gogarty's "Sindbad" poem into both *Ulysses* and *Finnegans Wake*. Shipwreck becomes a metaphor for the wrecked life; humpbacked Humphery, the "nowedding captain," is called a "wuntan whaal" (325.27, 31); the Gripes is "shapewrucked" (155.9), and Persse O'Reilly is "The unnamed nonirishblooder that becomes a Greenislender overnight" (378.10-11). Memories of "Sindbad" echo in Leopold Bloom's head as he falls asleep at the end of *Ulysses*, and the image of the shipwrecked sailor appears prominently in "Eumaeus" as well. Joyce did not forget the seemingly heartless manner in which Gogarty ridiculed his affliction, and it is for this reason, I believe, that he had his revenge by depicting Gogarty as his "betrayer," Malachi Mulligan.

Gogarty also appears in various disguises in *Finnegans Wake*. One can possibly read section I.2 of the *Wake*, which is full of allusions to Gogarty, and which ends in "The Ballad of Persse O'Reilly," as the story of how Joyce's friends ridiculed his misfortunes: "Hay, hay, hay! Hoq, hoq, hoq!" (33.27). Later, the broadcasting of HCE's misdeeds, suggests Joyce's feelings of betrayal at Gogarty's broadcasting the news of his malady.

After Joyce's death, Gogarty was to write: "To this day I am sorry for the thoughtless horseplay on such a hypersensitive and difficult friend" (*Mourning Becomes Mrs. Spendlove*

57). Given his jovial nature, Gogarty's reaction to Joyce's illness was to try to distract and amuse his friend rather than to sympathize with him. As he himself wrote, "I did my living best to cheer him and to make those thin lips of his cream in a smile. Very seldom I succeeded" (*It Isn't This Time of Year* 91).

Gogarty was a man who faced adversity with laughter. Years later, a friend of his, Ben Lucien Burman, describes a visit he paid to Gogarty in the New York hospital where he, Gogarty, was taken after collapsing from a heart attack: "We sat talking as casually as though we were at our intended dinner. He recited a few poems—his memory was phenomenal—and told me some funny stories he had heard in the last few days. He was so merry and laughed so much I began to worry that it might affect his heart. I tried to talk of something sad in the hope of making him less energetic. He was irrepressible" (*A Week End* 17). Two days later, Gogarty was dead. Because of his "irrepressible" sense of humor, his reaction to Joyce's illness, as to his own, had been one of laughter. Gogarty played Mercutio to his morose friend, which made Stephen Dedalus's nickname for him in *Ulysses*, "Mercurial Malachi," doubly, or perhaps triply, appropriate. It is ironic that with the passage of time, the "jejune Jesuit" also would find laughter the best way of coping with the burden of disease.

The correspondence between Joyce and Gogarty, with its references to mercury, to pox, to chancre, to Hunterian swellings, suggests that the illness that Joyce contracted in February of 1904 or earlier was syphilis.

Syphilis is a cyclical, or as Gogarty called it, an "intermittent" disease. The early symptoms soon disappear, with or without treatment, and the infected person appears to be "cured." Mercury, the standard treatment, had little or no effect on its course (Interview Kampmeier). Though the disease becomes dormant, the victim may still be infectious (or "ensectuous"—*FW* 29.30). Upon its awakening, he becomes "the Communicator."

For a young man only twenty-two years old, however, the disappearance of the initial symptoms after treatment would signify a "cure." Hence the rendezvous with Annie Langton. Joyce was treated for venereal disease in March of 1904. In June, he met Nora Barnacle. In August, according to Stanislaus's *Dublin Diary*, he began to talk "of the syphilitic contagion in Europe" that is "congenital and incurable" (51). In October, he eloped with Nora.

This was the beginning of the sequence of events in life that led to the themes of sin, punishment, and repentance that reverberate throughout Joyce's art. These themes were expressed through an elaborate, infinitely complex web of allusions, images, metaphors, and puns that can account for much of the difficulty of Joyce's later style. His illness was to provide both the context and subtext of his works.

At the end of *Portrait of the Artist,* when Stephen prays to "old father artificer," his namesake Daedalus, builder of wings and labyrinths, he does so as a young man ready to try his wings. Some time elapses and Stephen reappears in *Ulysses* as "lapwing," Icarus, the fallen man whose destruction is caused by his having wandered too far into forbidden realms. Now, having flown and fallen, Stephen identifies with Daedalus in his role of builder of labyrinths: "Remember Pasiphae for whose lust my grandoldgrossfather made the first confessionbox" (15.3865-66).

Confession, we are told by both clergymen and psychologists, is emotionally beneficial to the individual. In *The Psychology of Confession,* Erik Berggren, D.D., writes: "It is common human knowledge that talking about painful and disturbing memories or experiences which have lain on our minds unburdens us of them and affords a sense of relief. . . .The pressure [of guilt], as if by its own force, impels a release; the process may take the form of a powerful need to make disclosures, to speak openly about oppressive secrets. This need finds expression in two ways: either in personal confidences to a trusted friend or as a written description" (3). Theodor Reik, in *The Compulsion to Confess,* believes this compulsion to confess is unconscious, but he too asserts its positive emotional value: "We have noticed the psychic effect of confession upon the individual. Relief from the need for punishment and the hope for a new gain of love are not the only effects. The disintegrating of the personality is at least temporarily halted by the confession" (347).

There is ample evidence that the labyrinths which Joyce constructed are "confessionboxes." Stanislaus had pointed out in his Dublin diary, which Joyce was known to read, that the emotional relief which the sinner could obtain from the sacrament of Confession "also applies to those literary 'Confessions' and novels which the Church discountenances as most dangerous to morals" (153-54). Joyce, having cut himself off from the emotional relief usually afforded Catholics by the sacrament, sought through his art to absolve himself of a burden of guilt. But to do so, he used the impersonal third person narrator of fiction rather than the usual first person narrator of the confessional genre, thus for a time disguising the autobiographical nature of his later writings.

Joyce was well aware that in writing his confessions he was working within an established literary tradition. His library at Trieste abounded in works of this genre: *Les Confessions* of Jean-Jacques Rousseau, *La Confession d'un enfant du siecle* of Alfred de Musset, *Le Confessioni di un ottuagenario* by I. Nievo, *The Confessions of a Fool* by August Strindberg, and *La-Bas* by Joris-Karl Huysmans. He would surely also have read *The Confessions of Saint Augustine*, the prototype of the modern confessional novel, written by his patron saint, which Stanislaus mentions in his *Dublin Diary* having read; the two brothers often read the same books during this period of their lives. Joyce had also read the *Confession* of Saint Patrick. To Padraic Colum, he commented that Saint Patrick had waited too long to write his *Portrait of the Artist*, thus linking his own autobiographical work to Patrick's *Confession* (*The Joyce We Knew* 87). Likewise, Richard Ellmann's notes refer to a letter to Louis Gillet, dated 15 October 1931, in which Joyce indicated that Patrick's *Confessions* might be called "Portrait of Himself as an Old Man" (Tulsa).

Confessions are by their nature autobiographical. In a sense, because they deal with the inner rather that the outer life, they are also spiritual. Virginia Woolf, a sensitive reader, observed, "In contrast with those whom we have called materialists, Mr. Joyce is spiritual," but she also saw his method as "centered in a self which, in spite of its tremor of susceptibility, never embraces or creates what is outside itself and beyond" (*The Common Reader* 151). Acknowledging the autobiographical elements in Joyce's writing, T.S. Eliot, that most private of men, grants legitimacy to readers' curiosity into the details of Joyce's private life, "so that we may unravel the web of memory and invention and discover how far and in what ways the crude material has been transformed" (Preface to *MBK* viii). W.B. Yeats too recognized the personal nature of Joyce's fiction, calling *Portrait of the Artist* "disguised autobiography" (*Ltrs.* II: 356). Likewise, Stuart Gilbert noted the importance of autobiographical elements in Joyce's works: "He took the raw material of his art almost entirely from personal experiences, from his very wide reading, and from close observation of the little world of Dublin in which he spent his formative years. Thus, if we are to understand the background of his art—and this understanding is needed for its just appreciation—we cannot know too much about his life" (draft of article that appeared in Oct. 24, 1954 issue of *Saturday Review*, Stuart Gilbert Collection, U. of Texas).

In the early works, and in the Stephen sections of *Ulysses*, the disguise is thin, but until the publication of Joyce's letters and of Ellmann's biography, readers were not able to discern the extent to which Leopold Bloom was also a portrait of the artist, albeit in caricature. Even Ezra Pound was fooled, for while reading early drafts of *Ulysses*, he wrote Joyce to congratulate him on having finally created a character outside of himself (*Ltrs.* II: 423).

With *Finnegans Wake* the disguise became virtually impenetrable. However, James Stephens, whom Joyce asked to complete the work should he become unable, describes it thus: "I would call *Finnegans Wake* Joyce's autobiography: factual, imaginative, spiritual, and all curiously disguised; for Joyce was a secretive man, as we all are, and we all tell what we do tell with some precaution" (160). What is it, Stephens asks, that Joyce "would tell and would hide? and would still tell and hide again?" (159).

While writing *Finnegans Wake,* Joyce would send advance copies of chapters of his "Work in Progress" to people who knew him well, as if to see whether they could decipher his meaning before he ventured publication. He reported to Harriet Shaw Weaver the "advance press opinions" of family and friends who had read "Anna Livia Plurabelle." He wrote to Claud W. Sykes, "I will send you the opening pages of my new book . . . .If you can solve its ninetynineangular mystery will you please let me know" (*Ltrs.* I: 250). He told Ole Vinding that in that mass of shifting dreamstuff there was only one constant character: "If one were to speak of a person in the book, it would have to be of an old man" (Potts 149). That person could only have been himself. Paul Leon, the friend who acted as secretary to Joyce during the final years of his writing, also attests to the autobiographical nature of his works: "The time will come when the story of his life may be written, and it will be possible then to estimate to what extent he was pursued by misfortune, how much courage he needed to combat and dominate events. . . . Meanwhile, however, the student of the human soul should read attentively Joyce's writings in which it is mirrored, for Joyce made no distinction between actual life and literary creation. *His work is one long self-confession,* and in this respect he is akin to the greatest of the romantics" (emphasis added) (Potts 287).

For Joyce, however, given the embarrassing circumstances of his illness, and given his own reticent nature, confession could not be simple and forthright. As early as 1904 Stanislaus had noted in his *Dublin Diary:* "Jim is thought to be very frank about himself, but his style is such that it might be contended that he confesses in a foreign language—an easier confession than in the vulgar tongue" (110).

Consequently, some of Joyce's staunchest admirers, such as Harriet Shaw Weaver and Ezra Pound, were dubious about the literary value of *Finnegans Wake*. Weaver wrote him in February of 1927, "I am made in such a way that I do not care much for the output from your Wholesale Safety Pun Factory nor for the darknesses and unintelligibilities of your deliberately-entangled language system. It seems to me that you are wasting your genius" (Ellmann Collection, Tulsa). Ernest Hemingway expressed what many thought: "Joyce is a great man and now writes stuff that has to be read out loud by the author to have any point—and how he *could* write—" (Ltr. to Owen Wister, Library of Congress). Arthur Power, who had heard Joyce read aloud from "Work in Progress," later wrote, "I had not liked *Finnegans Wake* and had told him so. Indeed worse I thought, though I had remained silent about it, that he had wasted many vital creative years" (*The Joyce We Knew* 120).

Except for Paul Leon and Stuart Gilbert, most of those closest to Joyce seem not to have understood that his artistic purpose was autobiographical, but to some of his friends it was clear that he deliberately caused his readers to struggle. In her reminiscences, Sylvia Beach observed, "I think Joyce sometimes enjoyed misleading his readers" (185). Jacques Mercanton tells of watching Joyce and Stuart Gilbert rework a passage of *Finnegans Wake* that was "still not obscure enough," and Padraic Colum remembers being asked to suggest words that would be "more obscure" (Potts 214; *Our Friend James Joyce* 158). A letter from Paul Leon to Alexander Leon, of 30 June 1930, states (my translation): "And above all he [Joyce] writes in a manner which no one comprehends, nor is able to comprehend . . . . It was perfectly amusing to translate simple ideas into incomprehensible formulas and to believe that it was perhaps a masterpiece" (Tulsa).[5]

While Joyce was composing *Finnegans Wake*, Nora Joyce

complained that she was unable to sleep at night because "I go to bed and then that man sits in the next room and continues laughing about his own writing" (Giedion-Welcker in Potts 255). Like the devil, he spoke a language of his own called Bellsybabble, which he made up as he went along, all the while laughing to himself.

2
The Wandering Jew in *Ulysses*

Laughter for Joyce was a means of alleviating pain. "I am nothing but an Irish clown," he told Jacques Mercanton in a moment of dejection, "a great joker at the universe" (Potts 229). During the latter years of his life, when he poured out his woes over his poor health to Harriet Weaver, he wrote, "my ho head hawls and I feel as heavy as John McCormack but having some congenital imbicility in my character I must turn it off with a joke." About his children's illnesses he said, "I feel like an animal which has received four thunderous mallet strokes on the top of his skull. Yet in my letters to both my children and my daughter-in-law I keep up a tone of almost gay irresponsibility"; and while writing *Finnegans Wake*, "Perhaps I shall survive and perhaps the raving madness I write will survive and perhaps it is very funny. One thing is sure, however. *Je suis bien triste*" (Ltrs. I: 273, 366; III: 362). As his suffering intensified toward the end of his life, his writing became increasingly humorous. However, Stanislaus observed, "His wit, when it does crop up in his work, is sardonic" (*MBK* 242). Oliver Gogarty also recognized that Joyce was "a grim humorist" (Ltr. to Ulick O'Connor, U. of Texas).

Ulysses, Joyce's first truly comic work, is written from the ironic perspective of a man of experience who mocks both the intense, arrogant youngster that he once had been and the effete, flaccid husband he has become. W.B. Stanford has noted that Leopold Bloom at thirty-eight is the same age as Joyce during the writing of *Ulysses*, and that Stephen Dedalus at twenty-two is the age the writer had been when he departed from Ireland with Nora Barnacle (*The Ulysses Theme* 214). Whereas neither character is an exact depiction of the author, each parodies or mirrors some of his attributes at these stages of his life.

Much of Joyce's laughter in *Ulysses* is aimed at the distance between Stephen and Bloom, between his youthful aspirations and his actual attainments, at the deflation of pride and at the physical deterioration Bloom has undergone in eleven years' time. The irony of *Ulysses* lies not only in the disparity between Bloom and Homer's Odysseus, as some critics such as Darcy O'Brien and Hugh Kenner have indicated, but also in the differences between the Hellenic Odysseus, model of physical strength and courage and intellectual superiority that was Joyce's youthful ideal, and the medieval Ulysses of Dante, the fallen hero, the image with which Joyce later identified and upon which, I shall argue, he modeled Bloom. Significantly he gave his novel the Latin name.

Joyce first read *The Divine Comedy* in Italian when he was a college student. Dante's Ulysses is among the spirits of the damned, consigned to the upper circles of hell, a noble figure, enveloped in a horned-like flame, suffering eternal punishment because during his previous life he had wandered too far in search of forbidden knowledge and experience. Having sailed beyond the Straits of Gibraltar, beyond the Pillars of Hercules and the charted world, he was shipwrecked on the Mount of Purgatory, where he perished (Ellmann, *Consciousness* 29-30).

Gibraltar symbolized for Joyce a point of demarcation, the point at which he, like Ulysses (also like Sindbad the Sailor), had wrecked his life. Marxist critic Adolph Hoffmeister tells of a conversation in which the author described *Portrait of the Artist* as a picture of himself "from much earlier years. Before Gibraltar." When asked if he had been in Gibraltar, he lied: "As a language teacher. Then in Trieste, in Zurich, etc." (Potts 124). Ezra Pound in his *Pisan Cantos* (LXXIV) mentions, "Mr. Joyce also preoccupied with Gibraltar and the Pillars of Hercules" (*The Cantos* 25). *Finnegans Wake* also contains references to this point of no return (16.4; 128.36).

One of the recurrent themes in Joyce's novels is that of the hero who perishes because of wandering too far into forbidden realms, a mythic paradigm of the writer's own life. Life, Joyce told Samuel Beckett, is paradigm (Tulsa). We have seen, for instance, how Stephen Dedalus compares himself to Icarus, the disobedient son who flies too near the sun and then falls to his death in the sea: "Lapwing. Icarus. *Pater, ait.* Seabedabbled, fallen, weltering. Lapwing you are" (*U* 9.953-54). Though in his earlier life Stephen had felt "a lust of wandering in his feet that burned to set out for the ends of the earth" (*Portrait* 170), later in *Ulysses* he begins to recognize that he has wandered too far. In "Proteus," he imagines himself "walking into eternity on Sandymount Strand," and as he strolls out onto "unwholesome sandflats," he feels the ground "suck his treading soles" and he smells the stench of sewage. Moving out further toward the sea, he feels "his feet beginning to sink slowly in the quaking soil" and he admonishes himself, "Turn back" (3.18, 150, 268-9). Stephen is beginning to recognize that his association with Mulligan has been leading him astray: "His boots are spoiling the shape of my feet" (9.947). The crucial decision he faces at this stage of his life is whether to continue on his present course of dissipation.

Bloom too has undergone a change from earlier, happier days when he was: "precociously manly . . . . a fullfledged traveller for the family firm, equipped with an orderbook, a scented handkerchief . . . his case of bright trinketware . . . and a quiverful of compliant smiles for this or that halfwon housewife" (14.1046, 1050-53). Now, in middle age, he seems a sad old man: "Name and memory solace thee not. That youthful illusion of thy strength was taken from thee and in vain" (14.1074-75). Hugh Kenner has noted that "Ulysses returned to Ithaca had still his strength, Bloom at age 38 has fallen from his" (*Ulysses* 10).

Repeatedly we are told that he is not the man that he used to be. Any similarity he bears to the Greek hero Odysseus exists only in the past. At present, on 16 June 1904, he is more like Dante's Ulysses, a figure of fallen nobility, wearing horns, suffering the torments of the damned for having wandered too far in his previous life.

Dante's image of Ulysses as a punished sinner bears a strong resemblance to the medieval figure of the legendary Wandering Jew, who as punishment for his sin against Christ was cursed with eternal wandering. In his memoir of Joyce, Padraic Colum observed, "Ulysses and the Wandering Jew are different versions of the same character" (*Our Friend* 112). Significantly, though Joyce openly encouraged his readers to study the Homeric parallels in the novel, he left them to discover for themselves the allusions to the legend of the Wandering Jew. Early readers of *Ulysses* who wondered why Joyce chose to make his Odysseus a Jew failed to recognize the correlation between the theme of guilt and retribution associated with the legendary Jew and Bloom's wanderings in *Ulysses*, and the ongoing debate over the Jewishness of Bloom continues to focus on the religious and cultural identity of Bloom as opposed to his mythic identification (see Ch. 2 of McCarthy, *Ulysses: Portals of Discovery*).

In *The Consciousness of Joyce*, Richard Ellmann revealed that Joyce's Trieste library contained several literary variations of the legend of the Wandering Jew. The story originated in early Christian lore, an allegory fixing blame for the death of Jesus upon the Jewish people and attributing the destruction of Jerusalem and the dispersion of the Jews to God's punishment for their sin. Over a period of centuries the legend's meaning evolved. Thus, although the Wandering Jew is associated with Cain and the Antichrist as one of the great mythic sinners, he is not villainous. Unlike his counterparts, with the passage of time, the legendary Jew came to symbolize erring man ennobled by his suffering, thus resembling Dante's Ulysses.

Several times in *Ulysses,* Joyce directs the reader very deliberately to his use of the Wandering Jew legend in the novel. One pointed instance occurs at the end of "Scylla and Charybdis" when Buck Mulligan, looking at Bloom, says to Stephen, "The wandering jew . . . Did you see his eye? He looked upon you to lust after you. I fear thee, ancient mariner" (9.1209-11). Apart from the lewd suggestion inherent in Mulligan's remark, and the anti-Semitism, the passage points to the mesmerizing eye which is one of the attributes of the Wandering Jew.

Another passage in which Joyce calls the reader's attention to the legend occurs in "Cyclops," when the Citizen calls Bloom "Ahasuerus . . . . Cursed by God" (12.1667), Ahasuerus being the name of the Wandering Jew. In contrast with his method of incorporating the *Odyssey* into his novel, parodying blatantly both characters and episodes, Joyce uses the Wandering Jew legend more subtly. Images, verbal echoes, or allusions are interspersed throughout the work, frequently at great distances from each other, and bearing no chronological relationship to the legend. Joyce's method is the same as Bloom's for writing: "Pray for us. And pray for us. And pray for us. Good idea the repetition. Same thing with ads. Buy from us. And buy from us" (13.1122-24). As Bloom says, repetition is the whole secret. Thus we find in *Ulysses* recurrent echoes such as the wanderer's boots and staff, walking into eternity, the Blood of the Lamb, sin and punishment, the judgment day, and the announcement "Elijah is coming" resonating throughout the novel like Wagnerian *leitmotifs.*

Joyce had used the legend obliquely in an early essay he wrote on James Clarence Mangan, a nineteenth-century Irish poet. Here he depicts Mangan as a Wandering Jew figure in a description which could also apply either to Bloom or to himself: "Mangan has been a stranger in his country, a rare and unsympathetic figure in the streets where he is seen going forward alone like one who does penance for some ancient sin" (*Critical Writings* 76).

Before Carl Jung had formulated his theory of archetypes of the unconscious, Joyce had discerned archetypal patterns in literature and myth. Joseph Campbell, a disciple of Jung's, has commented extensively on Joyce's creation of a monomyth in *Finnegans Wake*, but actually this process had begun much earlier with *Ulysses*, where the dominant image is that of the wanderer, with whom Joyce, the exile, closely identified (see *Ltrs.* II: 48, 187, 255; III: 308, 333). Odysseus, the Hellenic wanderer, is conflated with the Wandering Jew, the Judeo-Christian, as well as with many other wanderers, literary or legendary, who appear in the work: Wandering Aengus, the Ancient Mariner, the Prodigal Son, Moses, Robinson Crusoe, the Flying Dutchman, the prophet Elijah, Sinbad the Sailor, Cain, Hamlet's father, and Shakespeare, whom Stephen calls the "passionate pilgrim" and about whom, John Eglinton says, "We know nothing but that he lived and suffered" (9.252, 360). However, just as other wandering characters in *Ulysses*—the blind stripling, the one-legged sailor, Denis Breen, Cashel Boyle O'Connor Fitzmaurice Tisdall Farrell, Kevin Egan—all are peripheral as compared with Bloom and Stephen, so are these other legendary figures of ancillary importance to Odysseus and the Wandering Jew, though they too represent variations of the theme of guilt and retribution.

The legend of the Wandering Jew has been repeated throughout European literature in innumerable variations.[1] This in essence is the story: on his way to Calvary, Jesus stopped to rest against the home of a cobbler named Ahasuerus, but the owner came out and angrily told him to move on. In some versions, he is supposed to have struck Jesus, thus his identification as a God-Smiter. Jesus in turn placed a curse upon the Jew, saying "I will move on, but so will you, until the end of time." Because of this curse, the cobbler was forced to leave his wife and children and wander into the world without destination, to keep moving until the day of judgment. As he wandered through the ages and through many countries, always speaking the language of the place in which he travelled, he was kept alive by his possession of a magical purse which perpetually replenished the coin needed to buy his daily bread. From this purse the Jew would share generously with others, this generosity being one of his distinguishing marks. He could also be recognized by his boots and staff, by his mesmerizing eye, by his recitation of the history of other times and places, by his appearance heralded by thunderstorms, by his infinite sadness. Like Bloom, he never laughed.[2] Repentant of his crime, the Wandering Jew was supposed to have acquired great wisdom from his suffering. After many years of wandering, he would periodically go to sleep, at the age of seventy or one hundred, and when he awakened, he would be rejuvenated, having returned to the same age at which he had sinned against Jesus, to take up his journey once again. (The legend thus suggests cycles of time analogous to Vico's theory of history.) Because he must wander until the end of time, the Wandering Jew is thought to herald the Day of Judgment. Like the Antichrist, and Judas, and Cain, he is supposed to appear when the last day is imminent. His Old Testament counterpart is the prophet Elijah, whose arrival was believed to herald the advent of the Messiah. In some versions of the legend, the Wandering Jew eventually returns home, centuries after leaving, only to find his family dead, his home destroyed. Symbolically this loss represents the historical destruction of Jerusalum.

Ulysses reverberates with references to the Wandering Jew which, because Joyce drew up no schema to guide us, the reader who is not closely familiar with the details of the legend might overlook. As with the characteristics of Odysseus, the traits of the legendary Jew are apportioned between Bloom and Stephen. For example, the wanderer's staff is transformed into Stephen's ashplant; Stephen also teaches history; the generosity of the Jew is reflected in Bloom's charity to the family of Paddy Dignam; Stephen is multilingual, whereas Bloom is bilingual; Bloom arrives at the Holles Street hospital in a thunderstorm; the coming of

Elijah is announced by the throwaway, by the parody of Bloom as Elijah at the end of "Cyclops," and in the parodic day of judgment in "Circe." Many of the traits of the Wandering Jew suggest biographical references to Joyce as well. He too carried a cane, was prodigal in his spending, was multilingual, was afraid of thunderstorms, was a wanderer all his life.

At the moment in the New Testament in which Jesus is sentenced to death (John 19:5), Pilate points to him and says to the Jews, "Behold the man" (Ecce homo) whom they have chosen to crucify instead of the thief Barrabas. This choice, according to Christians, is the sin of the Jews for which they were cursed by God. Joyce alludes to this biblical moment in "Lotus-Eaters" through Bloom's reference to "Ecce homo" (5.329), and in "Hades" and in "Wandering Rocks" through Simon Dedalus's and Ben Dollard's use of the epithet "Barrabas" (6.274; 10.950).

Just as the Wandering Jew returns home to find Jerusalem destroyed, wife and child dead, his former home a wasteland, so too does Bloom make mental pilgrimages back to Jerusalem, his ancestral home. In "Calypso," he imagines "A barren land, bare waste . . . .A dead sea in a dead land, grey and old. Old now. It bore the oldest, the first race . . . .The oldest people. Wandered far away over all the earth, captivity to captivity, multiplying, dying, being born everywhere. It lay there now. Now it could bear no more. Dead: an old woman's: the grey sunken cunt of the world" (4.219-28). In "Oxen of the Sun" he makes another journey: "silently the soul is wafted over regions of cycles of generations that have lived. A region where grey twilight ever descends . . . .She follows her mother with ungainly steps, a mare leading her fillyfoal . . . .They fade, sad phantoms: all is gone. Agendath is a waste land, a home of screechowls and the sandblind upupa. Netaim, the golden, is no more" (14.1079-87).

In his imagination, Bloom associates his ancestral home with his familial one. Agendath Netaim first appears in

Bloom's mind as a land of milk and honey, oranges and melons, the warmth of which he associates with the sensual world of Molly. Later, when he sees the little cloud (the significance of which we will examine later), Jerusalem is likened to an aged, barren woman, as Molly in time will be. After he has learned of Molly's intended infidelity, he sees Agendath as a wasteland. The vanishing mare and fillyfoal suggest the loss of wife and child. After her affair with Boylan, the image of Molly, like that of Agendath Netaim, is golden no more. The destruction of Bloom's ancestral home occurs also in his own. Significantly, he burns the flier upon his return.

Stephen Dedalus too is exiled from his home. At the end of "Telemachus" he says, "Home also I cannot go" (1.740). The place to which he refers is, like Bloom's, both real and symbolic. His earthly home is the overcrowded, undernourished household of his father, Simon Dedalus, where, if he returns, his pity and sense of responsibility towards his siblings will put an end to his career as a writer. To Stephen, however, the word *father* also signifies God-the-Father, in relation to whom he imagines himself a New Testament wanderer, the Prodigal Son. In "Circe," considering his dissipation, he says, "Filling my belly with husks of swine. Too much of this. I will arise and go to my [father's house]" (15.2495-96). Thus he acknowledges his need to return to his spiritual father. Bloom also alludes to the parable of the Prodigal Son when he says, "The stye I dislike" (15.2369), and he too thinks of Stephen in that guise: "grieved he also . . . for young Stephen for that he lived riotously with those wastrels and murdered his goods with whores" (14.75-76). When he asks Stephen, "Why did you leave your father's house?" the young man replies with a telling pun, "To seek misfortune" (16.252-53).

For Stephen, as for the young James Joyce, home had been devastated by the death of his mother, following which he had entered a period of dissipation, drinking and whoring with Mulligan and his medical student friends, probably in an attempt to alleviate his grief over his loss. This behavior only increased his feelings of estrangement from family, society, and religion, making it impossible for the Prodigal Son to return to his Father's house.

Both Stephen and Bloom share the quality of the Wandering Jew as God-Smiter in the sense that both are estranged from the faiths of their childhood. In *Ulysses* this idea is conveyed symbolically through images of light and darkness. Stephen smashes the lamp, and in "Proteus" he turns his back to the light in order to write. In Joyce's favorite gospel, that of St. John, light is equated with life and with Christ. According to August Suter, "St. John for him was THE evangelist. He often quoted the text: 'At the Beginning there was the Word [*sic*]'" (Ellmann Collection, Tulsa). During Joyce's lifetime, the opening verses of St. John were read aloud in the Roman Catholic Mass as the last gospel: "In the beginning was the Word, and the Word was with God, and the Word was God. He was in the beginning with God. All things were made through Him, and without Him was made nothing that has been made. In Him was life, and the life was the light of men. And the light shines in the darkness and the darkness grasped it not." Joyce used this light imagery in the hell and damnation sermon in *Portrait of the Artist*, when the priest depicts the sufferings of the sinner: "the worst damnation consists in this that the understanding of man is totally deprived of divine light and his affection obstinately turned away from the goodness of God" (127). In *Ulysses*, Stephen, who has rejected the faith of his childhood, inverts the gospel of St. John in his imagination to identify himself with "dark men," with heretics and with Lucifer, who gave forth "a darkness shining in brightness which brightness could not comprehend" (2.158, 160). In "Nestor," when the old bigot Mr. Deasy voices traditional Christian prejudice against the Jews, his words echo the imagery of the gospel of John: "They sinned against the light . . . . And you can see the darkness in their eyes. And that is why they are wanderers on the earth to this day" (2.361-63). Stephen rejects the old man's anti-Semitism, but not the correlation of darkness with sin, for in "Proteus" he thinks, "Darkness is in our souls . . . . Our souls, shamewounded by our sins, cling to us yet more, a woman to her lover clinging, the more the more" (3.421-23).

Like Stephen, Bloom too is associated with darkness and dresses in black, but in his greater wisdom he remembers that "dark men" is a name given to blind men. Bloom too is a nonbeliever, but not so much a God-Smiter as Stephen. He recognizes the human need for light: "People afraid of the dark . . . . Light is a kind of reassuring" (13.1069-71). In "Circe" Bloom retrieves the lamp that Stephen has smashed, and in "Ithaca" he lights a candle for them both (Davis 127).

Nevertheless, Bloom is estranged from Judaism, the faith of his forefathers, just as Stephen is from Catholicism. He regrets that in his youth he had found the teachings of the Jewish faith foolish; now in middle age he feels remorse "Because in immature impatience he had treated with disrespect certain beliefs and practices" (17.1894-95). In "Circe" the apparition of his father addresses him as "my dear son Leopold who left the house of his father and left the god of his fathers, Abraham and Jacob" (15.261-62). Bloom's family has followed the historical pattern of other Jewish families in Ireland who succumbed to Christianity because of economic pressures. Many of these converted Jews later became Freemasons, as did Bloom, because the secret rituals of that organization correspond to similar ritualistic elements of Judaism (Hyman 59). Joyce draws upon these historical facts about the Jews in Ireland when Bloom recalls the reasons why his father abandoned the ancient faith: "They say they used to give pauper children soup to change to protestants in the time of the potato blight. Society over the way papa went to for the conversion of poor jews. Same bait. Why we left the church of Rome" (8.1071-74).

Hence the references in *Ulysses* to the Old Testament figure of Esau, who sold his birthright for a bowl of pottage. When Stephen says, "I am tired of my voice, the voice of Esau. My kingdom for a drink" (9.981), the allusion indicates that already he suspects that in giving up his faith for sexual and intellectual freedom, he may have made a bad bargain. In the essay "Ireland, Island of Saints and Sages," which Joyce had written in Trieste in 1907, he used the metaphor of Esau to describe the Irish people: "although the present race in Ireland is backward and inferior, it is worth taking into account the fact that it is the only race of the entire Celtic family that has not been willing to sell its birthright for a mess of pottage" (*Critical Writings* 166). Even this early in his life it seems that Joyce was beginning to recognize that a person who in his youth discards his cultural heritage, which is transmitted from one generation to another through religious teachings, frequently in maturity will repent his haste.

Bloom feels the loss of his half-remembered Judaic heritage; even those aspects that had seemed foolish to him in his youth now seem "Not more rational than they had then appeared, not less rational than other beliefs and practices now appeared" (17.1903-4). As we see in "Ithaca," his efforts to substitute rational and pseudo-scientific thought for faith have proved cold comfort when he has been faced with disasters. Bloom is a deracinated modern Jew, cut off from his historical and cultural past, ignorant of the faith of his fathers, a misfit in the churches and rituals of Christianity. His relationship to Jerusalem and Judaism is analogous to what Stephen's, and Joyce's, will be in middle age to Ireland and Catholicism.

As we have noted, another wanderer frequently alluded to in *Ulysses* is the Old Testament prophet Elijah, who evaded death by ascending to heaven in a whirlwind (II Kings 2:11) and returned, according to folklore, to wander over the earth bringing comfort and hope to mankind. Old Testament prophets associated the reappearance of Elijah on earth with the coming of the Messiah and the fulfillment of the prophecies of the Messianic Age. This prediction in the Old Testament is analogous to the Christian belief that the appearance of the Antichrist and/or the Wandering Jew would herald the Apocalypse and the second coming of Christ. In *Ulysses* the throwaway announcing the coming of Elijah precedes the apocalyptic fantasies of "Circe."

Significantly, the return of Elijah is foretold in the Book of Malachi (4:5, 6) (Blackmur 104): "Look, I will send you the prophet Elijah before the great and terrible day of the Lord comes. He will reconcile fathers to sons and sons to fathers, lest I come and put the land under a ban to destroy it." Joyce associates Bloom with Elijah when he parodies the prophet's ascension in a fiery chariot with Bloom's hasty departure from Barney Kiernan's in the final scene of "Cyclops." And he causes Elijah to reappear after the End of the World as the evangelical preacher on the fantastic Day of Judgment that occurs in "Circe." Furthermore, he gives the name of the Old Testament prophet who foretells the coming of Elijah to Malachi Mulligan, the first character we encounter in the novel.

Malachi in Hebrew means "my [God's] messenger," a role that Joyce underscores with "Mercurial Malachi" (1.518), thus identifying the Hebrew messenger with the Hellenic one (Blackmur 104). (We have already seen another reference to mercury which Joyce associated with Gogarty.) The message that Malachi gives to the Hebrew people is a warning to render unto the Lord the honor and fear, the tribute and reverence which is His due, to return to the path of righteousness, lest a curse of banishment be laid upon them.

Malachi Mulligan's words nettle Stephen's conscience, taunting him for refusing to pray at the bedside of his dying mother, and for panning Lady Gregory's book after she had helped him. He also taunts him about venereal disease. Stephen's resentment towards Mulligan comes from the fact that his words stir memories of pain, guilt, and shame that Stephen would like to forget.

When Stephen sees Mulligan enter the library in "Scylla

and Charybdis," he speaks the words of the evil King Ahab to the prophet Elijah, "Hast thou found me, O mine enemy?" (9.483) (I Kings 21:20). For Ahab, a worshipper of false gods and murderer of an innocent man, the coming of Elijah signifies that he is about to meet his doom. The Biblical allusions point to the source of Stephen's guilt, his feeling of having sinned against God and of having killed his mother. The riddle he keeps repeating about the fox that buried its grandmother seems associated in his mind with the superstition that wolves dig up the corpses of murder victims. The original riddle's answer is, "The fox burying his *mother* under a holly tree" (Gifford, Ulysses *Annotated*, 33). Though rationally Stephen knows that his mother died of cancer, he cannot avoid feeling that he has contributed to her death by defecting from her religion.

The Old Testament prophecies of Malachi also point to the source of Bloom's guilt, for the prophet admonishes the Israelites for being unfaithful to their wives: "And what does the one God require but godly children? . . . If a man divorces or puts away his spouse, he overwhelms her with cruelty, says the Lord of Hosts the God of Israel." Because for a long while, perhaps for eleven years, Bloom has not had sexual intercourse with Molly, he feels that he has contributed to her infidelity, causing her to seek sexual gratification with another partner. His sin, like that which Stephen attributes to Shakespeare, is "like original sin, committed by another in whose sin he too has sinned" (9.1008). In "Ithaca," when we see Molly "denoted by a visible splendid sign, a lamp," we recognize that Bloom too has sinned against the Light (17.1178).

In *Ulysses* the theme of guilt and retribution reaches its climax in the parodic Day of Judgment that is enacted in "Circe." Here we see Stephen, dressed as Cardinal Sin, "suffering the agony of the damned," dancing the *danse macabre* with prostitutes (the dance of death suggesting the risks of venereal infection), adamantly refusing to obey the warnings of his conscience that appear to him in the spectre of his dead mother (15.2679). He smashes the lamp of faith, to have Bloom discover later that "Only the chimney's broken" (the phallic connotations again emphasizing the physical destruction that occurs in the brothel) (15.4285). In "Circe," Bloom also confronts the Sins of the Past and the source of his guilt, which is associated with Molly and the death of his son Rudy. As the "Adorer of the adulterous rump," he too has worshipped false gods (15.2839). Unlike Stephen, he admits his wrongdoing, "Yes. Peccavi! [I have sinned.] I have paid homage on that living altar where the back changes name," and he repents, crying out, "Moll! I forgot! Forgive! Moll!" (15.3405, 3150). At this point, we hear again the motif which recurs in Bloom's thoughts throughout the day, "I have sinned! I have suff[ered]" (15.3215; 5.373; 8.125). As the Wandering Jew, Bloom's punishment for his sins is to spend a day wandering through the streets of Dublin while his wife has an affair with another man. Through his suffering he gains wisdom. At the end of "Circe," he too encounters the source of his guilt, the spectre of his little son Rudy, for whose death he holds himself responsible.

The death of the infant Rudy is a major crux of Joyce's *Ulysses*. The loss of this child, some eleven years before the story begins, has blighted the lives of the parents. From Bloom's reminiscences we learn that since the child's death, he and Molly have no longer had a good sexual relationship: "Twentyeight I was. She twentythree. When we left Lombard Street west something changed. Could never like it again after Rudy" (8.608-10). In "Ithaca" it is revealed that after Rudy's death, "there remained a period of 10 years, 5 months and 18 days during which carnal intercourse had been incomplete, without ejaculation of semen within the natural female organ" (17.2282-84). During the day of June 14, 1904, both parents think about the death of the infant, Bloom dwelling on it repeatedly. His reflections indicate the burden of guilt he carries over his son's death:

"Our. Little. Beggar. Baby. Meant nothing. Mistake of nature. If it's healthy it's from the mother. If not from the man" (6.328-29). To ascertain the cause of the infant's death, he has gone so far as to acquire a copy of *Aristotle's Masterpiece*, a book containing pictures of deformed babies, a book which Molly finds disgusting.

Joyce offers no direct explanations as to why the baby died, nor why the couple's conjugal relations have ceased, nor why Bloom permits the wife that he loves to have an affair with another man, nor why after so many years Bloom still is haunted by the memory of his son. As Morris Beja has noted, it seems a matter of "gross oversimplification . . . to explain their abstinence entirely or merely as a primitive form of birth control" ("The Joyce of Sex" 259). Under usual circumstances, one would expect a couple that had lost a much wanted child to try to have another, but the opposite is true of Leopold and Molly. Throughout the text of *Ulysses*, Joyce strews numerous hints, pointing to illness, from which we can infer that good reasons exist for Bloom's unusual behavior.

In Joyce's "epic of the body," as E.L. Epstein has perceptively noted, "The fear of bodily death . . . pursues Bloom through the book" (81). Joyce well knew from his own experience that at no time does the body assume such paramount importance as in the state of illness. What I shall posit here is the idea that much of Bloom's otherwise incomprehensible behavior can be explained if we assume that Joyce's many references to venereal disease in *Ulysses* (which Vernon Hall and Burton Waisbren have already established) point to the idea that Bloom is a sick man.[3] If Bloom is infected with such a disease, that fact could account both for the child's death and for the father's consequent burden of guilt. Joyce reinforces the theme of guilt over the death of Rudy through verbal echoes not directly linked to Bloom, such as the homophonous phrase "Childs murder" in "Oxen of the Sun," and the description in "Circe" of the death of Mary Shortall's baby, which occurred because the mother was infected with the pox. Furthermore, Bloom's illness could explain why he wanders on the fourteenth of June instead of interfering with his wife's assignation with Blazes Boylan.

I do not ask my readers to rely upon my authority for a diagnosis of Bloom's malady. Harder evidence can be found in the notebook that Joyce used in preparation for writing *Ulysses*. Under the "Penelope" section is an entry in his own hand indicating "L. B. had clap" (V. A.2, p. 3, SUNY Buffalo). Another of the notebooks (VI. B.19 p. 172) includes an entry "syphyllis" (*merci* Chris Bjork).

When Bloom contemplates Blazes Boylan keeping his appointment at 7 Eccles Street, the sound "Clappyclapclap" echoes through his head. In "Oxen of the Sun" and in "Penelope," the clap of thunder sounds like the crack of doom (*Ulysses* 388-89, 726). *Clap* is a slang term for gonorrhea, but I will argue here that Joyce uses the word to encompass venereal diseases generally, including syphilis. It is important to understand that syphilis and gonorrhea are not a matter of either/or. Frequently, as in the case of the eighteenth century English physician John Hunter, they are "impure," or mixed; in other words, a person can contract both simultaneously.

Repeatedly through the day, Bloom's thoughts turn to venereal disease. One of the more subtle instances is when he passes an apothcary and thinks, "Poisons the only cures. Remedy where you least expect it. Clever of nature" (5.483-84). One disease for which poisons were the only cure was syphilis, which, before the advent of penicillin, was treated primarily with mercury and arsenic. These remedies were not used for the treatment of gonorrhea, nor commonly for anything else (Goodman, *Pharmacological Basis of Therapeutics* 1050-95). Elsewhere, more overtly and repeatedly, Bloom notices or thinks about poxy prostitutes, injected with dark mercury, and fears the infection they might spread.

As we noted earlier, since the death of Rudy, Bloom has undergone enormous physical changes, changes which suggest deterioration beyond the normal process of aging for a man of thirty-eight. Ned Lambert tells his drinking buddies, "You should have seen Bloom before that son of his that died was born." Molly remembers how "very handsome" he had been before their engagement; and Bloom, recalling Molly's kissing him on the Hill of Howth, reflects sadly, "Me. And me now" (12.1650-51; 18.208-9; 8.917). His transformation, like the changes of his family name from Virag to Bloom (and later in fantasy to Henry Flower), suggests a loss of masculinity, a loss underscored by his seemingly effete acquiescence in Molly's affair with Boylan, and also by his metamorphosis in "Circe" into the "new womanly man," who, we are told, is "practically a total abstainer" (15.1803-4). Molly bemoans her fate, "living with him so cold never embracing me except sometimes when hes asleep the wrong end of me" (18.1400-1401). Though Bloom has considered a rendezvous with his penpal Martha, and though he masturbates over the spectacle provided by Gerty McDowell, with his wife, we are told, he can accomplish only "An approximate erection" (17.2238).

Although Joyce gives no direct explanation for Bloom's motivation in permitting Molly to keep her assignation with Blazes Boylan, throughout the novel he strews verbal hints that the husband is impotent (*pace* Morris Beja).[4] References to the spoutless teapot, to the keyless citizen, to "U.P.: up" and "Who's getting it up?", to "waiting and coming," to "Horn. Have you the? Haw haw Horn," to "What's home without/ Plumtree's Potted Meat?/Incomplete./With it an abode of bliss" all suggest the theme of impotence.[5] In "Lotus-Eaters," the image of the gelded horses with "a stump of black guttapercha wagging limp between their haunches" prefigures that of Bloom's own "limp father of thousands, a languid floating flower" (5.218, 571-72). Even the title of the chapter "Lotus-Eaters," which ends with this flower image, implies the destruction of masculine powers. So does Bloom's paraphrase of Martha's letter, "Angry tulips with you darling manflower punish your cactus if you don't"

(5.264). Much of the phallic imagery in the novel, a source of risqué humor, points to Bloom's incapacity. For instance, twice when he imagines himself in the role of Rip Van Winkle (a variation of the Wandering Jew), his attention focuses upon Rip's "rusty fowlingpiece" and "His gun rusty with the dew" (15.3160; 13.1116). The sight of the fireworks display in "Nausicaa" inspires him with this analogy: "My fireworks. Up like a rocket, down like a stick" (13.894-95).

Other characters in the novel seem to know what is wrong with Bloom. They hint at his impotence through the names they assign him: pinprick, the prudent member, his own and his only enjoyer. The medical students jibe, "Has he not nearer home a seedfield that lies fallow for the want of the ploughshare?" and Bella Cohen asks him outright, "What else are you good for, an impotent thing like you?" (14.929-30; 15.3127). Surprisingly, everyone seems to understand Bloom's problem except Molly herself, who believes "he came somewhere I'm sure by his appetite anyway love its not or he'd be off his feed thinking of her so either it was one of those night women . . . or else if its not that its some little bitch or other he got in with . . . because he couldn't possibly do without it that long so he must do it somewhere" (18.34-36, 44-45, 76-77).

Perhaps it is an effort to cure his impotence that causes Bloom to look for a younger partner in Martha Clifford. And because of his inability with his wife, he has also allowed Molly to take another partner. There are suggestions in *Ulysses* that Bloom has not only permitted Molly's infidelity but has actually encouraged it. In "Circe" he is taunted by The Sins of the Past because "In five public conveniences he wrote pencilled messages offering his nuptial partner to all strongmembered males" (15.3034-35), and in "Ithaca," he shows an old photograph of Molly to Stephen Dedalus, encouraging the younger man to meet her.

Though rationally Bloom views Molly's infidelity as a matter of physical necessity, emotionally he is nevertheless devastated by her behavior. At the end of the day, in "Ithaca," he endeavors to control his jealousy by viewing her actions with scientific detachment, as a process "of adaptation to altered conditions of existence, resulting in a reciprocal equilibrium between the bodily organism and its attendant circumstances, . . . significant disease" (17.2191-4). A significant disease which causes impotence would explain why Bloom tolerates Molly's adultery, and also why Molly would be tempted to commit adultery.

Like his creator, Leopold Bloom had been a sexually active young man who visited prostitutes. In the maternity hospital, Bloom remembers his first encounter with a whore, Bridie Kelly:[6] "She is the bride of darkness, a daughter of night. She dare not bear the sunnygolden babe of day. No, Leopold! . . . That youthful illusion of thy strength was taken from thee—and in vain. No son of thy loins is by thee" (14.1073-6). Bloom expresses great hostility toward prostitutes, calling Bella Cohen "Pox and gleet vendor" (15.3498). Indeed, *Ulysses* contains many references to the evils that befall man because of woman.

Bloom worries that Stephen should "waste his valuable time with profligate women who might present him with a nice dose to last him his lifetime" (16.1554-56). Just as Bloom is warned about the dangers of Nighttown by the spectre of his grandfather Virag, who advises him on various home remedies for venereal diseases, so too does Bloom try to warn young Stephen against the possibility of infection, but the young man ignores the warnings. Thus, as the Wandering Jew falls asleep at the end of the novel, his younger incarnation trudges off into the night to repeat the errors of his symbolic father. In one of his Zurich notebooks, Joyce wrote, "the son's life/repeats the/father's. He does/not see it" (VI. B. 3, SUNY Buffalo). We can surmise that in time Stephen will come to resemble his symbolic father, because the sins of his present life are the same as those of his father's past. In his notes Richard Ellmann wrote that "Yesterday shall be tomorrow" is the point of *Finnegans Wake*, but this cyclical theory of time also applies to the events in *Ulysses*, both on a realistic and on a mythic plane (Tulsa).

If Bloom did indeed contract venereal disease in a brothel, and if this disease has caused both his own impotence and the death of the child Rudy, then we must ascertain what kind of venereal infection would account for both of these results. Either gonorrhea or syphilis could cause infant mortality, but only *tabes dorsalis*, a form of neuro-syphilis, is associated with impotence.[7] This particular type of syphilis attacks the dorsal nerve roots of the spine which control the lower extremities of the body. It affects the sexual organs, the sphincter muscles (recall Bloom's fascination with sphincters), the movement of the legs and feet, and sensations of pain in the lower part of the body, including the gastric system (Cecil *Textbook of Medicine*, 7th ed. 400-403; Frank A. Elliott, *Clinical Neurology*, 2nd ed, 318-323; Raymond Adams, *Principles of Neurology* 644-45).

If Bloom does suffer from *tabes dorsalis*, then he ought to manifest other symptoms of the disease besides impotence. Because the distinguishing sign is a peculiar gait, the common name given to *tabes dorsalis* is "locomotor ataxia," or as the prostitute Florrie calls it, "Locomotor ataxy" (15.2592). One medical textbook describes it thus: "The legs are kept far apart to correct the instability, and patients carefully watch the ground and their legs. As they step out, the legs are flung abruptly forward and outward, often being lifted higher than necessary. . . . The body is held in a slightly flexed position, and the weight is supported on the cane that the severely ataxic patient usually carries" (Adams 73). In "Aeolus" the newsboys mock Bloom's funny walk, "Taking off his flat spaugs and the walk," and Lenehan imitates him with a "mazurka in swift caricature across the floor on sliding feet" (7.448-51). In "Aeolus" Bloom is described as having "strode on jerkily," and in "Circe" as having blundered "stifflegged" out of the path of an oncoming trolley (7.994; 15.191). When the motorman calls out to him, "Hey, shitbreeches, are you doing the hattrick?", Bloom appreciates the cleverness of the insult, "Quick of him all the same. The stiff walk. True word spoken in jest" (15.195, 206-7).

Another symptom of *tabes dorsalis* is loss of control of the bladder. In "Lestrygonians" Bloom notices "Dribbling a quiet message from his bladder came to go to do not to do there to do," a dilemma that Joyce mocks later with a pun (echoing Gogarty's letter to Dr. Walsh) when Bloom tells Cissy Caffrey that "his waterworks were out of order" (8.933-34; 13.550-51).

The disease also causes loss of control over the bowels, sometimes causing constipation, at other times incontinence. Bloom has both. In "Calypso" we learn that he has had to purchase cascara sagrada (a laxative) to relieve his constipation, and in "Circe" we are told of the episode of the bucket, again the scatological humor masking embarrassment and pain: "A large bucket. Bloom himself. Bowel trouble. . . . Gripe, yes. Quite bad. A plasterer's bucket . . . . Suffered untold misery . . . . Crucial moment. He did not look in the bucket. Nobody. Rather a mess" (15.929-34).

Nerve damage resulting from *tabes dorsalis* also causes "lightning" or "lancinating" pains in the extremities and "gastric crises" (vomiting and sharp pains in the abdominal area). Bloom suffers from pains in his legs and stomach. He carries in his pocket a "Spud again[st] the rheumatiz" (14.1480-81). At one point, he attributes spasms to having run too fast, and at another, he remembers "That awful cramp in Lad Lane. Something poisonous I ate" (15.207-8). In "Circe" he complains: "I have felt this instant a twinge of sciatica in my left glutear muscle." (15.2782-83). Joyce's choice of words in "Oxen of the Sun" suggests that Bloom suffers from lightning pains: "Parallax stalks behind and goads them, the *lancinating lightnings* of whose brow are scorpions" (emphasis added) (14.1089-90). In August of 1908, Stanislaus parrots this terminology in his Trieste diary: "his [Jim's] eyes are well but he still feels rheumatic lancinations" (Tulsa). The words *lancinating* and *lightning pains* occur repeatedly in medical textbooks, referring specifically to *tabes dorsalis.*

Likewise in medical textbooks, the terms *acquired* and *congenital* are used in reference to syphilis, the latter referring to the disease being transmitted to the child before birth. In the maternity hospital, Buck Mulligan attributes the causes of sterility to "defects congenital" or to "proclivities acquired" (14.671-72). And while the medical students discuss the causes of infant mortality, Bloom sits by, silently listening: "Still the plain straightforward question why a child of normally healthy parents and seemingly a healthy child . . . succumbs unaccountably in early childhood (though other children of the same marriage do not) must certainly . . . give us pause. Nature . . . has her own good and cogent reasons for whatever she does and in all probability such deaths are due to some law of anticipation by which organisms in which *morbous germs* have taken up their residence . . . .[emphasis added] tend to disappear at an increasingly earlier stage of development" (14.1273-82). The "morbous germs" of either gonorrhea or syphilis can cause an infant to die. Gonorrhea causes an infected mother to miscarry. Syphilis may cause the child to be aborted, to be stillborn, or to be born alive but infected. However, not every child born to an infected mother will itself necessarily be infected; thus Milly does not appear to have any signs of illness.[8] Sometimes a child is fatally afflicted and dies soon after birth; sometimes the germs are present only in the central nervous system and make their appearance years later. Bloom comments that the midwife Mrs. Thornton "knew from the first poor little Rudy wouldn't live" (4.418-19). An infant mortally afflicted with syphilis would have visible signs of disease (Kampmeier, *Essentials* 413; "Late and Congenital Syphilis" 36-37).

For a child to contract syphilis before birth, the mother must also be infected. Bloom gets his facts a little muddled when he thinks of the death of Rudy: "If its healthy it's from the mother. If not from the man" (6.329). This seeming misapprehension would in a sense be true, however, if the father blames himself for the child's illness or death because he has contracted venereal disease from a prostitute and then infected his wife.

Such a possibility seems to lurk in Molly's mind. She thinks about a man she knows who meets with "some filthy prostitute then he goes home to his wife after that" (18.1424-25).[9] Molly also indicates her awareness of Bloom's having visited painted women in the past, but she is not yet conscious that he may have infected her. A woman recently infected with syphilis might show no visible sign of the disease because the initial chancre frequently occurs internally. Should she become pregnant shortly afterwards, her secondary symptoms would be milder than otherwise because of her stronger immunities during pregnancy; the symptoms might even go unnoticed (*Syphilis, A Synopsis* 45, 50; Kampmeier, *Essentials* 398-99). Gonorrhea also affects a woman internally, often causing vaginal discharge (Interview with Dr. J. Howard Young, gynecologist). In *Ulysses* the question of whether Molly has been infected is crucial, because if she has not, then Rudy's death would have to be attributed to causes other than venereal disease. In "Calypso," Molly's "soiled drawers" appears prominently on her bed. In "Circe," the image is repeated, "Soiled personal linen, wrong side up with care. The quoits are loose. From Gibraltar by long sea, long ago" (15.3288-89). Molly's dirty linen and the quoits made loose from travelling beyond Gibraltar, like Bloom's "waterworks" out of order, are, I believe, metaphors suggesting physical maladies. In "Penelope" we learn that Molly is beginning to suspect her health when she wonders, "who knows is there anything the matter with my insides or have I something growing in me getting that thing like that every week when was it last I Whit Monday yes its only about 3 weeks I ought to go to the doctor" (18.1149-51).

In women, gonorrhea and other sexually transmitted diseases can necessitate hysterectomy (Brandt 15). Nora Joyce had one in 1929. In earlier times, according to Joyce's correspondence, she also had stained drawers. The symptoms in *Ulysses* point not only to Leopold and Molly, but also to Jim and Nora. Shortly after the pair left Dublin in 1904, after Joyce had been "cured" of his venereal infection, Nora became pregnant with their first child, Giorgio, who was born in July of 1905. Two years later, in July of 1907, their second child, Lucia, was born. At the time of her birth, Joyce was seriously ill, and, according to Richard Ellmann, was hospitalized in Trieste (*JJ* 262). Stanislaus believed and wrote to the family that Jim had had rheumatic fever, a diagnosis which Stannie himself was the first to pronounce and which he reiterated many times. According to Stanislaus's Trieste diary, contrary to Ellmann's account, Joyce was not hospitalized but was treated at home both for rheumatic fever and for his first bad attacks of uveitis (eye disease). However, years later, in 1916 when Joyce was in Zurich, he wrote to Ezra Pound that his eye attacks were "a consequence of malarial fever" which he had contracted in Rome (Yale, Beineke Library).[10] This inconsistency suggests either that Joyce could not remember what kind of fever he had had, nor when, or that he was, as Stannie once described him, "the worst liar I know" (*Dublin Diary* 55). This illness could have been a relapse of an earlier venereal infection about which Stannie had not been informed.

During the years 1906 through 1908, at which time Stanislaus records Joyce's physical ailments in his diaries in minute detail, Joyce suffered, along with each attack of uveitis, a variety of recurrent symptoms: indigestion, stomach pain, back pains, neuralgia, "rheumatic" pains "which shift from spot to spot" (a characteristic of lightning pains), weakness, and exhaustion. As early as December 28, 1904, he had written to Stanislaus about cramps in his stomach and problems with his vision (*Ltrs*.II: 75). At this time, it seems, he first began to wear glasses. Syphilis often causes uveitis and glaucoma, the eye diseases from which Joyce suffered (Smith and Nozik, *Uveitis: A Clinical Approach to Diagnosis and Management* 179, 181), and the constellation of accompanying symptoms which Stanislaus describes are all compatible with *tabes dorsalis* (sources listed earlier). These symptoms were to intensify, with periods of remission, throughout the course of Joyce's life.

In 1908 the Joyces lost a child, their third, by miscarriage. According to Ellmann, who quoted from Stanislaus's Trieste diary, Joyce carefully examined the foetus, "whose truncated existence" he said to Stanislaus, "I am probably the only one to regret" (*JJ* 268-69). It seems surprising that a father who was unable to support the two young children that he already had would wish for a third. During Nora's last pregnancy, again according to Stannie, she was taking an "ugly arsenical medicine" before meals, as prescribed by her physician (Trieste diary, Tulsa). At this time, arsenic would have been used experimentally in the treatment of syphilis. By 1909, just one year later, it had become the standard treatment, replacing mercury, the earlier remedy (Pusey 58). It was especially important to treat infected women who were pregnant in an effort to protect the unborn child (Cecil, 7th ed. 383).

Joyce himself suffered from many of the symptoms of *tabes dorsalis* that Bloom exhibits. His peculiar walk was commented upon by almost everyone who knew him. Letters to his brother also reveal problems with constipation in November of 1906 (*Ltrs.*II: 187, 189). Repeatedly he wrote to friends about the sciatica and "rheumatic" pains he suffered in his legs and about the digestive ailments that plagued him. Both Richard Ellmann and Brenda Maddox suggest that Joyce lost sexual interest in women while he was still a rather young man. In its later stages, *tabes dorsalis* can cause perforated ulcers, the illness from which Joyce died (Cecil, 7th ed. 402). The disease is progressive if not treated with penicillin (discovered in 1941, the year of Joyce's death), and if the victim does not succumb to other causes, ends in paralysis, a major theme in Joyce's writings.

And so we see that the theme of sin and guilt, crime and punishment, pain and loss, which occurs on both the mythic and physical levels in *Ulysses,* parallels the physical and emotional ordeal that Bloom and Joyce undergo. Venereal disease was considered God's punishment for sexual sins. Just as the mythic or religious or literary allusions form a coherent pattern pointing to guilt, so too do the scatological or physiological references point to a disease that carried with it a burden of shame. Because so many of the scatological references are very funny, occuring in puns and jokes, we can easily overlook the grimness underlying the humor. As Molly Bloom observes, "there's many a true word spoken in jest" (18.775). Most frequently, Joyce's laughter is directed at Leopold Bloom—at his blunders, at his Bloomisms, at his minutely described bodily functions. Bloom's plight is an allegory, a mythologizing, of the author's own experiences. *"Il se promene lisant au livre de lui-meme,* don't you know, *reading the book of himself"* (9.114-15). By achieving a mythic perspective on his own suffering, Joyce was able to escape the dangers of being overwhelmed by self-pity and despair, perhaps by madness. For him laughter provided catharsis, purgation. Like Stephen, "He laughed to free his mind from his mind's bondage" (9.1016). We as readers, however, need to recognize that frequently what we are laughing at is a story of human pain. If my assumptions are correct, then *Ulysses* is no paean to the joys of life and love, but rather a lament over the follies of youth and their devastating consequences. Joyce's humor is the dark and bitter laughter of self-satire.

3
Epics of the Body

Joyce described *Ulysses* to Frank Budgen as an "epic of the body," a term he was to use frequently in reference to the work (*Making of* Ulysses 21). He wrote to Carlo Linati that *Ulysses* is "an epic of two races (Irish and Israelite) and also the cycle of the body," thus indicating two major planes, mythical and physical, on which his work operates (*Ltrs.* I: 146). To Jan Parandowski he repeated, "*Ulysses* is more an epic of the body than of the human spirit . . . . for too long were the stars studied and man's insides neglected. An eclipse of the sun could be predicted many centuries before anyone knew which way the blood circulated in our bodies" (Potts 158-59). In the schema he drew up for Carlo Linati, Joyce assigned a different organ of the body to each chapter. But until recently, most of Joyce's critics, devoting their energies to the mythic or linguistic, psychological or political implications of the novel, have paid little attention to the idea of *Ulysses* as an epic of the body. Those who have considered the question seem to assume either that Joyce's references to the body are less important than those to the development of the soul (Epstein, "James Joyce and the Body" 75), or that his emphasis of the importance of physicality should be equated with an advocacy of sexual freedom (Ellmann, *Ulysses on the Liffey* 174-75; Brown 126-42, 153). However, as we examine Joyce's references to the body, frequently occurring in scatological jokes, not only in *Ulysses* but in his other works as well, we find that far from lauding sexual freedom, Joyce is pointing to the correlation between carnal sins and physical illness.

Many physiological terms occur in Joyce's works, terms which commentators have usually interpreted as metaphor:

hemiplegia and paralysis represent the spiritual stagnation of Irish civilization, or of the Roman Catholic Church (Brandabur in *Dubliners* 337); prostitution represents the selling of the spiritual for the material (Kaye, *James Joyce Miscellany, 2nd Series* 89); sexual intercourse represents the relationship of mind to reality (French 53); masturbation is a "repulsive symbol of Irish paralysis, sterility, and corruption" (D. O'Brien 161); blindness "is not physical or the result of disease, but comes from a cataract of the mind which they do not recognize" (Cixous 293); and "physical control is the paradigm for the psychological and moral patterns of the book" (Schechner 127). Such criticism, in my opinion, by thus converting physical references into symbol, obscures rather than clarifies the literal meaning of the work. This tendency toward symbolic reading, which Joyce did encourage, has prevented readers from observing in *Ulysses* the correlation between spiritual and physical malaise. In Joyce's world, as Epstein has noted, body and soul are indeed connected.

T.S. Eliot once applied the phrase "two plane" to Joyce's work, a phrase that Joyce himself liked very much (*Ltrs.* III: 83). Though actually *Ulysses* operates on many planes, not just two, the term is useful in delineating its highest and lowest levels. The highest, the mythic, provides universal analogues for Joyce's realistic characters and lends a spiritual dimension to their domestic crises. Leopold Bloom is more than just any Jew who wanders through Dublin; he is the archetypal Wandering Jew whose sufferings are eternal. Mythic and literary allusions often direct the reader's attention to serious themes; however, frequently they also provide one side of a pun or metaphor, the other side of which operates at a lower level, the comic, which is rooted in physicality, in scatology, in sacrilege. For Joyce, no bodily function is too private or too embarrassing to be included; no source of allusion too sacred to be burlesqued, turned into a pun or *double entendre*. As we have seen in the preceding chapter, many of the jokes about bodily functions refer to symptoms of illness. Likewise many of Joyce's literary puns or allusions emphasize the body, both in *Ulysses* and also in *Finnegans Wake*. As we shall see, Joyce devised a complex symbolism for those later works, some of which is borrowed from Gogarty, so that he could write about his obsession with the body diseased.

For instance, when in "Lotus-Eaters" we see Bloom imagining his naked self stretched out in the bathtub, he pronounces over himself the words of consecration from the Roman Catholic Mass, "This is my body." By combining the sacred and the profane in two sides of a single joke, Joyce—James the Punman, he once called himself—not only shocks and amuses us, but also points to the transformation undergone by Bloom's body and his "limp father of thousands" (*Ltrs.II*: 157; *U* 5.566, 571).

A more subtle example of Joyce's use of allusion is the appearance of the Nameless One among Bloom's accusers in "Circe." "The Nameless One" is the title of a poem by James Clarence Mangan, a poem which young Joyce would recite at social gatherings (Sheehy, *The Joyce we Knew* 33). A romantic rendition of the Wandering Jew legend, Mangan's shipwrecked wanderer is a poet who, like Coleridge's Ancient Mariner, feels compelled to recount his experiences and sufferings. The poem reverberates with many themes that recur in *Ulysses*:

> Go on to tell how, with genius wasted,
> Betrayed in friendship, befooled in love,
> With spirit shipwrecked, and young hopes blasted
> He still, still strove . . . .
>
> And tell how now, amid wreck and sorrow,
> And want, and sickness, and houseless nights,
> He bides in calmness the silent morrow
> That no ray lights.
>
> And lives he still, then? Yes! Old and hoary
> At thirty nine, from despair and woe,

> He lives enduring what future story
> Will never know.
> (Frank O'Connor, ed. *A Book of Ireland*)

The Nameless One, like Leopold Bloom, is a man prematurely old and physically broken.[1]

The transformation scene of "Circe" is another example of Joyce's use of allusion, in this case of multiple allusions, to underscore spiritual decline and physiological change. Bloom's transformation into a pig-like woman, sinking on "all fours, grunting, snuffling, rooting" at Bella Cohen's feet, signifies his emasculation and his descent into bestiality as a consequence of having falsely worshipped the "adulterous rump" (15.2839). The degradation of the Prodigal Son, to whom Stephen has earlier alluded, leads him also to a pig sty. The porcine transformation further recalls the transformation of Odysseus's men into swine when they fall under the spell of the nymph.

Joyce possibly had a third literary allusion in mind as well. While he was composing "Circe," he wrote to his friend Frank Budgen: "Moly is the gift of Hermes (Mercury), god of public ways and is the invisible influence (prayer, chance, agility, presence of mind, power of recuperation) which saves in case of accident. This would cover immunity from syphilis (συφιλιs = swinelove?)" (*Ltrs.* I: 147). Then later he explained further: "I always thought the etymology was syn philais (together with loving, connected with it) but a man named Bradley says the other [swinelove]" (*Ltrs.* I: 149).[2]

Joyce's source, Bradley, may have directed him to the origin of the name syphilis, a sixteenth-century poem "Syphilis Sive Morbus Gallicus," written in Latin by Girolamo Fracastoro, an Italian physician and poet. In this poem a mythological shepherd named Syphilis, having offended the gods by worshipping his king in their stead, is punished by Apollo with a terrible transforming disease, the symptoms of which are described in terms medically

accurate for that time (Spink 307-8; Pusey 33). Dr. William
Allen Pusey concluded that the name Syphilis which
Fracastoro gave to his hero, probably derived "from συς
(swine) and φιλος (lover)." Because the transformations both
of Bloom and of the shepherd occur as a punishment for
worshipping false gods, it is tempting to conclude that Joyce
must have known the poem, but harder evidence is lacking.
The only indication that he might have known it is from his
use of the term "morbous germs," seeming to echo the title
of Fracastoro's poem, in a passage (quoted in Chapter 2) of
"Oxen of the Sun." What is certain is that Joyce did associ-
ate Bloom's swinishness with the disease. Nowhere are the
venereal implications of the novel more explicit than in the
brothel scene.

Joyce directs us to the theme of venereal infection through
a multitude of references, most frequently to syphilis. In
the opening chapter, as we have noted, Mulligan jokingly
tells Stephen that an acquaintance has said that Stephen is
suffering from general paralysis of the insane. Bloom recalls seeing advertisements for a cure for clap posted in the
urinals of Dublin by Hy Franks, "Post no bills. Post 110
pills," and wonders whether Boylan could infect Molly
(8.101). Both Bloom and Molly imagine the army and navy
"rotten with disease" (5.72, 18.1425). The Citizen mocks
King Edward by saying "There's a bloody sight more pox
than pax about that boyo," and he denigrates English civilization by calling it "syphilisation" (12.1400, 1197). (Actually, syphilisation was a nineteenth century medical theory
that people could be immunized against syphilis. See Quetel
112-14.) The medical students use "a stout shield of
oxengut" less for contraception than for protection against
the "foul plague Allpox," and they recite a parody of a
prayer from the Mass, asking to avoid the "snares of the
poxfiend . . . . Thrust syphilis down to hell" (14.1537, 1543).
In the brothel of "Circe," the prostitutes discuss the fate of
poor Mary Shortall who was infected with pox by "*Jimmy*

Figure 1. *Treponema pallidum,* the spirochete that causes syphilis (from U.S. Government Printing Office).

Pidgeon in the blue caps," and Lynch, looking at a whore, declares, "And to such delights has Metchnikoff inoculated the anthropoid apes," Metchnikoff being the first doctor to infect a non-human species with syphilis for purposes of research (emphasis added) (15.2578, 2590; Pusey 66). Another prostitute, Florrie, replies knowingly, "Locomotor ataxy" (15.2592), a reference to *tabes dorsalis.* Bloom carries a potato as a cure for rheumatism and protection against pestilence, and he carries soap, which, if applied to the skin soon enough, will kill the spirochete, *Treponema pallidum,* that causes syphilis. (See figure 1.)

Many of the scatological jokes in *Ulysses* refer to symptoms of venereal disease, some with reference to Bloom, some to Stephen, some to other characters, such as Reuben J. Dodd, or the blind stripling, or Denis Breen, or Cashel Boyle O'Connor Fitzmaurice Tisdall Farrell, whose name seems to encompass half of Ireland, as if to imply that everywhere the afflicted man looks, he sees the horror of infection, and indeed, that infection is everywhere. Many of the same symptoms are also suggested in the imagery and puns of *Finnegans Wake.* In November of 1906, Joyce wrote to Stanislaus, "I presume there are very few mortals in Europe who are not in danger of waking some morning and finding themselves syphilitic" (*Ltrs.* II: 192). The effect in

Ulysses is similar to that of the Breughel painting "Carnival and Penitence," depicting maimed bodies and blighted souls. Mrs. Breen watches the demented Cashel wandering down the street and thinks, "Denis will be like that one of these days" (8.304), and Molly remembers Mrs. Breen's telling her that her husband would sometimes go to bed with his muddy boots on "when the maggot takes him" (18.223). (Again, the image reflects early medical theories, predating the science of microbiology, that syphilis was caused by tiny worms in the body. See Quetel 79.) If my supposition is correct and Bloom too suffers from the maggot, only at an earlier stage of development or in a different form, then Molly's assertion that Bloom at least does not behave that way is loaded with irony. The image of the maggot recurs frequently in *Finnegans Wake*. Finn is called "Macnoon maggoty mag!" and "as a murder of corpse [matter of course] when his [HCE's] magot's up he's the best berrathon sanger in all the aisles of Skaldignavia [scalding knavia]" (254.32).

Until 1943, when doctors realized that the newly discovered drug penicillin would effectively cure syphilis, the disease had ravaged Europe for centuries, since the late fifteenth century when it was believed to have been introduced from the New World by Columbus's sailors. (Though some medical authorities now discredit this story, it was still held true by Dr. William Allen Pusey in his *The History and Epidemiology of Syphilis*, published in 1933.) Joyce refers to the supposed New World origin of syphilis in the opening paragraphs of *Finnegans Wake*: "Sir *Tristram, violer d'amores*, fr'over the short sea, had *passencore rearrived from North Armorica*" to fight his "*penisolate war*" (emphasis added) (1.4-6). At one level, I read this passage to suggest that the misfortune (*tristesse*) that spoils or violates lovemaking (violer d'amores) and destroys penises had not yet (*pas encore*) arrived from North America. A later passage reinforces the idea of the New World origin of disease, "He sent out Christy Columb and he came back with a jailbird's unbespokables in his beak," again alluding to the unspeakable infection with which Columbus's men supposedly returned in their "beaks" (496.30). Another reference to the New World origin of syphilis also occurs in *Ulysses* in Bloom's stump speech in "Circe": "Sir Walter Raleigh brought from the new world that potato and that weed, the one a killer of pestilence by absorption, the other a poisoner of the ear, eye, heart, memory, will, understanding, all. That is to say, he brought the poison a hundred years before another person whose name I forget brought the food" (15.1356-60). Bloom, as usual, confuses his facts but arrives at a mode of truth nevertheless. His reference to "that weed" seems to mean tobacco, which does not directly poison eye, ear, memory, will, understanding, and the carcinogenic properties of which were not yet understood in the 1920s. Syphilis, however, does "poison" all of the areas of the body and personality that Bloom names, and its symptoms were well documented by this time. I interpret the weed referred to in the above passage as another of Joyce's metaphors for disease.

In 1924 Joyce twice wrote to Harriet Weaver using the term "poisoned" to describe his own physical condition, telling how in years past he had been "underfed, overworked, ill dressed, with septic poisoning gradually undermining my health," and how "the labour of *Ulysses* must have undermined my strength. I was poisoned in more ways than one" (*Ltrs.* I: 215, 216). We have already observed in Chapter 1 that poison is one of the metaphors by which victims of venereal disease describe their misfortune. Furthermore, "poison" is a term frequently applied to syphilis in the early literature on the subject (Quetel 25, 52, 54, 69). In the *Wake*, "Slow poisoning" is associated with the "saxy luters [sexy looters] in their back haul of Coalcutter [black hole of Calcutta]" (492.14)—i.e., with the vaginas of whores—and HCE is said to have given "his best hand into chancerisk [chancre-risk], wishing him with his famblings [family] no end of slow poison" (582.4).

Before the advent of penicillin, syphilis was treated with

heavy metals. Throughout the early decades of this century, mercury was the recommended treatment, either by inunction, by oral consumption, or by injection. It probably had little or no effect on the course of the disease (Interview with Dr. Rudolph Kampmeier). Bismuth and iodides were also used. In 1907 a doctor named Paul Ehrlich produced a compound of arsenic called Salvarsan, the 606th drug of a long series of arsenical preparations with which he had experimented until he found one that was both effective against the invading bacteria *T. pallidum* and still capable of being tolerated by the human body (Quetel 142). Buried deep in *Finnegans Wake* is the pun "*salver's inn*keeping" (emphasis added) (345.20) and the number "six hundred and six" (478.9), which corresponds to the number of the compound which was effective (Goodman and Gilman 946-99; Moore 59). Both mercury and arsenic being highly toxic, the treatment of the disease often involved side effects almost as bad as the disease itself. Among other things, mercury caused the teeth to loosen and fall out (Quetel 61-62). In "Proteus" Stephen thinks, "My teeth are very bad. Why, I wonder" (3.94). Joyce too had very bad teeth, which had to be completely extracted early in 1923 (*JJ* 543).

As I have noted in the "Prologue," after treatment with arsenic there was the possibility of severe reaction, the Herxheimer reaction, from a flare-up of spirochete activity in the lesions of late syphilis. In order to minimize the dangers of such a reaction, doctors would administer bismuth before giving arsenic treatments (Goodman and Gilman 967, 978). *Finnegans Wake* contains a reference to "Big Maester Finnykin" as "this prime white arsenic with bissemate alloyed, martial sin with peccadilly," the pun I hear being "mortal sin with peccadillo/pecker dilly" (577.4).

As we have already seen, correspondence with Oliver Gogarty suggests that Joyce was administered mercury in 1904, at that time the standard treatment for syphilis. Gonorrhea was treated with other metals (Goodman and Gilman

851-61; 1050-95). Later in his life, Joyce was also treated with arsenic, a treatment that was not commonly used for any malady other than syphilis. To my mind, this treatment constitutes virtual proof of his doctors' diagnosis of the disease. In October of 1928 he wrote both to Harriet Weaver and to Valery Larbaud that he was being given injections of arsenic for three weeks, the standard treatment for syphilis during the 1920s. To Larbaud he added: "They examined 'all the internal organs of the beast' and his blood pressure and found everything normal except his nerves" (*Ltrs.* I: 270-71; III: 182). (In *tabes dorsalis* gastric crises and lightning pains are caused by lesions in the spinal cord, hence by nerves.) Thus, having been treated probably with mercury and certainly with arsenic, and with his wife having been administered arsenic during her last pregnancy, Joyce would readily have seen "poison" as a logical metaphor for disease.

In *Ulysses* Bloom's thinks about poisons on several occasions. We have already noted the reference to the apothecary in "Lotus Eaters." In the brothels of "Circe" also he is acutely aware of prostitutes who have been treated with mercury. At one point he sees "a sinister figure . . . a visage unknown, injected with dark mercury" (15.212). The apparition of his grandfather Virag warns Bloom against the dangers of contracting venereal disease. Pointing to one prostitute, he notes, "The injection mark on the thigh I hope you perceived? Good." Looking at another, he comments, "Beware of the flapper and bogus mournful. Lily of the alley. All possess bachelor's button [chancre] discovered by Rualdus Colombus. Tumble her. Columble her. Chameleon" (another reference to the New World origin of syphilis) (15.2340).

To become a chameleon is to undergo what Stephen calls a "seachange," for the spirochetes infiltrate the body of their host through the bloodstream. In *Finnegans Wake*, H.C. Earwicker, the Host, sleeps while "his bluidstreams acrawl" (74.14). In *Ulysses*, Bloom, who in "Ithaca" is repeatedly called "the host," ponders [3] "the myriad minute entomological organic existences concealed in cavities of the earth . . . of microbes, germs, bacteria, bacilli, spermatozoa . . . of the universe of human serum constellated with red and white bodies " (17.1059-64). Stephen, in "Scylla and Charybdis," thinks, "Through spaces smaller than red globules of man's blood they creepycrawl" (9.86). Another symbolic reference to blood is made by the old sailor in "Eumaeus" who is "bad in the eyes" because "Sand in the Red Sea done that" (16.1674, 1678). Similar imagery occurs in *Finnegans Wake* where we are told of "the drowning of Pharoah (Humpheres Cheops Exarchas) and all his pedestrians . . . completely drowned into the sea, the red sea" (387.26; 62.21). Shaun reviles Shem because "He has encaust in the blood. Shim! I have the utmost contempt for. Prost[itute] bitten!" (424.8).

Syphilis enters the human body through a single port of entry called the initial lesion or chancre, which can occur on any mucous membrane or break in the skin exposed to the infecting organism. The chancre forms after a period of incubation lasting from ten to ninety days (*Syphilis: A Synopsis* 22-25; Kampmeier, *Essentials of Syphilology* 112). Bloom's grandfather Virag puns on Huguenot/huge knot, "But possibly it is only a wart" (15.2375). When the prostitute Zoe feels the potato in Bloom's pocket and declares, "You've got a hard chancre," he replies, "Not likely" (15.1304, 1306). The ambiguous answer could mean that he does not have the disease, or it could indicate that his case has progressed beyond the early stages when a hard chancre would occur. Bloom's contact with prostitutes such as Bridie Kelly have taken place in the past, the inference being not the very recent past.

Joyce uses the metaphor of the "hidden wound" to indicate the initial lesion of syphilis.[3] In *Finnegans Wake* Joyce writes: "how slight becomes a hidden wound? Solwoter he wash him all time bigfeller bruisy place blong him . . . . It will paineth the chastenot in that where of his whence he had loseth his once for every . . . . and the Tarara Boom decay" (247.22-28). The lesion is suggested also in the pun "Thanks ever*sore* much, *Point*carried!" [emphasis added] (304.5), and made specific in "A pipple [pimple] on the panis [penis], two claps on the cansill, or three pock pocks cassey knocked on the postern!" (538.13).

We are never told directly that Bloom has been infected with venereal disease, but Joyce makes several references to metaphorical "wounds" that strongly suggest such a possibility. In "Oxen of the Sun," the inflated language describing Bloom's bee sting implies a far more serious injury than an insect bite (which in Renaissance literature was a metaphor for sexual intercourse, *merci* Georgia Christopher), and the treatment he is given suggests inunction of mercury, which was applied in doses as strong as the body could tolerate before signs of poisoning occurred: "And there came against the place as they stood a young learning knight yclept Dixon. And the traveller Leopold was couth to him sithen it had happed that they had had ado each with other in the house of misericord where this learning knight lay by cause the traveller Leopold came there to be healed for he was sore wounded in his breast by a spear wherewith a horrible and dreadful dragon was smitten him for which he did do make a salve of volatile salt and chrism as much as he might suffice" (14.125).

Later, on the way to Burke's, when one of the medical students asks Dixon, "Got a pectoral trauma, eh, Dix?", referring to Dixon's patient, he replies, "Pos fact. Got bet be a boomblebee whenever he was settin sleepin in hes bit garten . . . . Buckled he is" (14.1472). The passage spoken by Signor Maffei in "Circe" also suggests wounding, treatment by inunction and metamorphosis: "It was I broke in the bucking broncho Ajax with my patent spiked saddle for carnivores. Lash under the belly with a knotted thong. Block tackle and a strangling pulley will bring your lion to heel, no matter how fractious, even *Leo ferox* there, the Libyan maneater. A redhot crowbar and some liniment rubbing on the burning part produced Fritz of Amsterdam, the thinking hyena" (15.709).

The theme of the fatal wound is also sounded in Stephen's disquisition on Shakespeare in "Scylla and Charybdis," a wound that critic William Schutte has interpreted as psychic, but which is clearly located in the genitals. In this passage we see the metaphor of the wound followed by that of poison:

> Belief in himself has been untimely killed. He was overborne in a cornfield first . . . and he will never be a victor in his own eyes after nor play victoriously the game of laugh and lie down . . . . No later undoing will undo the first undoing. The tusk of the boar has wounded him there where love lies ableeding . . . . The soul has been before stricken mortally, a poison poured in the porch of a sleeping ear. But those who are done to death in sleep cannot know the manner of their quell unless their Creator endow their souls with that knowledge in the life to come. (9.455, 469)

Stephen's rendition of the life of Shakespeare, as Schutte has noted, bears many similarities to the life of Bloom. He too, according to Dixon, has been poisoned in his garden, "wounded where love lies ableeding . . . done to death in sleep" while still in the vigor of youth. Only in the life to come, after his metamorphosis, does he learn the "manner of his quell."

The story about Bloom/Shakespeare is repeated in *Finnegans Wake* in one of the rumors that circulates about HCE: "It was the first woman, they said, souped him, that fatal wellesday, Lili Coninghams, by suggesting him they go in a field" (58.28). HCE, called "the common or ere-in-garden castaway" (62.19), is likewise the "Vakingfar sleeper, mono-fractured by Piaras UaRhuamhaighaudhlug, tympan founder" when "They finally caused, or most leastways brung it about somehows, (that) the pip of the lin (to) pinnatrate inthro an auricular forfickle" (310.8). The often-repeated ear imagery also applies to Finn, whose demise is attributed, among other causes, to the "bitch bite at his ear" (5.35).

The wound causes a metamorphosis. That Bloom's body has undergone a change is evident in "Eumaeus" when he leads Stephen by the arm, and Stephen thinks "he felt a strange kind of flesh of a different man approach him, sinewless and wobbly" (16.1723). HCE also goes through a transformation when "after a goodnight's rave and rumble," he "was not the same man"; like the Wandering Jew, after sleep he had been "rejuvenated" (41.13-15). HCE is the reincarnation of Finn, just as Stephen is of Bloom.

In all likelihood, Stephen, like Bloom, has already undergone a seachange, one less advanced. Thinking of his lust for women, he remembers how he had prayed to the Virgin Mary that he might not have a "red nose" (3.129). At first the reader thinks of the red nose of the alcoholic, but on reflection realizes that this would not warrant prayers to the Virgin. However, prayers to the Virgin Mary for protection against the disease became customary following the outbreak of syphilis in Europe (Quetel 14).[4] The reference to the red nose recurs in the poem "Epilogue to Ibsen's *Ghosts*" that Joyce wrote, in which the infected Captain Alving expresses envy of Haakon who is lucky enough to enjoy himself with prostitutes, "Spreeing and gleeing as he goes . . . / Without a pimple on his nose" (Yale, Joyce Collection). The image also occurs in *Finnegans Wake*: "This is Canon Futter with the popynose. After his hundred days' indulgence"; likewise, Shem the Penman wrote by the light of "his gnose's glow" (9.19, 182.4).

In "Proteus" the changes which Stephen observes suggest signs of decay and death. Syphilis was called a "protean disease" by sixteenth century doctors because of its variform nature (Quetel 77). The body of the drowned man, which Stephen sees in his mind's eye, has undergone the metamorphosis of death, but the specific changes he imagines, the "spongy titbit" in the trouser fly, the "leprous nosehole snoring to the sun," and the "brown eyes saltblue," all are mutations that can be caused by syphilis in the living body (3.477-82). Stephen fears the changes that may be in store for himself. The sight of the bloated carcass of the dog causes him to recall Mulligan's words: "Ah, poor dogsbody! Here lies poor dogsbody's body" (3.351). In contemplating the dog's death, he visualizes his own. Stephen's preoccupation with death in this chapter is underscored by his identification with Hamlet, who also indulges in morbid speculations.

Stephen is afraid as well that he is losing his eyesight. Imagining how it would feel to be blind, he shuts his eyes and uses his ashplant to guide his way. (In "Lestrygonians," after helping the blind stripling to cross the street, Bloom too imagines being blind.) Stephen's comment before opening his eyes: "I will see if I can see" (3.26). Later he thinks of the scene from *King Lear* when blind Gloucester tries to commit suicide (3.149).

Bloom too fears for Stephen's future. The sight of the young man "brought to mind instances of cultured fellows that promised so brilliantly, nipped in the bud of premature decay, and nobody to blame but themselves" (16.1183). He is, of course, thinking of his own youth as well as Stephen's. He sees in the young man the "predestination of a future" and hears "the traditional accent of the ecstasy of catastrophe" (17.780, 786).

From the initial chancre of syphilis, *Treponema pallidum* enters the bloodstream and, in the case of some unlucky individuals (8 to 10 percent of those untreated), the central nervous system, thereby causing neurosyphilis. Approximately 66 percent of the people infected never have symptoms beyond the initial chancre and the secondary symptoms; a healthy, well nourished person might have enough natural resistance to fight the infection; Joyce, however, was not well nourished. According to W.G. Fallon, as a boy, Joyce was sometimes given food by Mrs. Sheehy and the rector of Belvedere because he was so hungry, and according to Stanislaus's diary, Jim and Nora frequently went undernourished in Trieste (Ellmann's notes and Trieste diary, both at Tulsa). But the remaining 34 percent of syphilitic victims will either suffer infectious relapses for up to four years after infection and/or go into a period of latency which can last for many years, followed by serious tertiary lesions which occur usually in the second and third decades of the disease, but which can occur earlier (*Syphilis: A Synopsis* 22-25.)[5] Through the bloodstream *T.pallidum* can invade any organ of the body and form tiny lesions of the blood vessels or tissues, "the lessions of experience" and "the blessons of expedience" (puns on *lessons* and *lesions* and Fr. *blessures*, meaning wounds) as Joyce calls them in the *Wake* (436.20; 156.4). Eventually these form the tertiary lesions of syphilis called *gummata* (sing. *gumma*). These large erosions of tissue can occur on the skin, in bones, in the eyes, in the liver or aorta, or in the central nervous system. (For a complete medical description of the disease, see Russell L. Cecil, *A Textbook of Medicine*, 7th and 16th eds., 1948, 1982; or Rudolph Kampmeier, *Essentials of Syphilology.*)

In medical textbooks, the cyclical nature of syphilis is illustrated by a line graph curving up and down, which corresponds metaphorically to Joyce's (or Vico's) cyclical theory of history: thus stages of disease also represent various cycles of time. As we have seen in *Ulysses*, different characters are infected at various stages of the disease. In "Circe" the watchmen (alluding to Jean Cocteau's *La Machine Infernale*) sound the warning of pending doom: "The bomb is here . . . . Infernal machine with a time fuse" (15.1197, 1199). In *Finnegans Wake* the periods of incubation and dormancy of the disease are symbolized by Finn's and Earwicker's sleep: "Humph is in his doge [doze]. Words weigh no no more to him than raindrips to Rethfernhim. Which we all like. Rain. When we sleep. Drops. But wait until our sleeping. Drain. Sdops" (74.16).

Of the three possible types of neurosyphilis, Joyce mentions two by name in *Ulysses*. Paresis, also know as "general paralysis of the insane," was once a leading cause of insanity. In the *Wake* the Mookse says to the Gripes, "Parysis . . .

belongs to him who parises himself" (155.16). *Tabes dorsalis*, formerly called "locomotor ataxia," affects the dorsal roots of the spinal cord, and its symptoms, as we have noted, are seen primarily in the lower extremeties of the body. Earwicker's extremeties are "extremely so" (74.15). As I have shown in the preceding chapter, most of the symptoms of this particular form of neurosyphilis are to be found in Bloom, some in Stephen, and many in Joyce himself.

In 1975 an article appeared in the *Irish Medical Times* by a Dr. F.R. Walsh (who bears the same surname as Dr. Mick Walsh who treated Joyce in 1904) in which the author states that Joyce's father had boasted of contracting syphilis some ten years before his marriage and had treated himself, he claimed, with "carbolic." (Among the home remedies that Bloom's grandfather Virag recommends for venereal disease is "caustic.") Dr. Walsh goes on to suggest, and this idea is repeated in the popular biography of Joyce by Stan Gebler Davies, also published in 1975, that Joyce's medical problems stemmed from congenital syphilis. In 1930 Joyce wrote to Harriet Weaver that one of his doctors had suggested that his eye troubles were the result of congenital syphilis (*SL* 348). Actually, it is highly improbable, perhaps impossible (depending on which medical authority one consults), that a man could transmit syphilis to his wife, and hence to their children, ten years after his infection. Once the disease has become latent (after the first four years), he is no long contagious (Interview with Dr. Rudolph Kampmeier). Of course, it is possible for the husband to have been infected more recently, or for the wife to have contracted the disease as a consequence of an extramarital affair, but no evidence exists to suggest infidelity on the part of Joyce's mother.

Furthermore, congenital syphilis is not a third generation disease (Interview with Dr. Rudolph Kampmeier). Had Joyce suffered from congenital syphilis, it is improbable, perhaps impossible, that he could have passed it on to his children, yet, as I will show, he lived in fear and dread that he had done so. Moreover, Joyce's eye ailments (severe uveitis, synechiae, cataracts, and glaucoma) are more commonly associated with acquired syphilis than with late congenital syphilis.

If Joyce did have syphilis, it is far more likely that he contracted it in the brothels of Dublin or Paris, both of which he frequented from a very young age, than that he got it from his mother and father. In 1902 during his first trip to Paris, he wrote to his mother about suffering a strange malaise: "I received both your letters and see that I have alarmed you very much. My curious state has been followed by an equally curious weariness which is however painless" (*Ltrs.* II: 21). Lassitude is one of the symptoms of early syphilis (Quetel 77).

Pusey, writing in America in 1933, reports the incidence of syphilis among prostitutes to range "from 38 percent to almost universal existence among old prostitutes," and he says that European statistics indicate that syphilis was more prevalent in European cities than American (77, 78). Claude Quetel, who devotes an entire chapter of his *History of Syphilis* to "The Pox and the Prostitute," writes: "Few whores escape the pox. The estimated percentage of prostitutes who were syphilitic varied between 30 and 70 according to the time, the place, and the generosity of the statisticians; but from this point onwards there was a tendency to argue that every prostitute would inevitably be infected with syphilis after a certain number of years" (219).

Tabes dorsalis develops within four to thirty years after the time of infection and usually progresses very slowly, so that very little change can be observed in the individual from one year to another. Eventually, however, if the victim does not die of other causes, it leads to paralysis (see Frank A. Elliot, *Clinical Neurology*, 2nd ed, 318-23; Raymond D. Adams, *Principles of Neurology* 644-45).

As we have seen, the distinguishing symptom of *tabes* is an unusual, unsteady gait, such as Bloom seems to manifest. One of the peculiarities of this condition is that "The incoordination is greatly exaggerated when the patient is deprived of visual cues, as in walking in the dark. Most patients, when asked to stand with feet together and eyes closed, show greatly increased swaying or actual falling (Romberg's sign)" (Adams 73). In *Ulysses* Stephen also is unsteady on his feet. During his "dance of death" in "Circe," the manner in which he totters when he closes his eyes (15.4152) is suggestive of the Romberg sign described above. (In "Circe," the basic technic is lack of motor control.) When Stephen loses his balance and is caught by Bloom to prevent his falling, he explains, "My centre of gravity is displaced. I have forgotten the trick" (15.4433). Later he is still "a bit weak on his pins" (16.1717). Perhaps he carries his ashplant out of physical necessity, not merely as an affectation. Mulligan tells Haines, in reference to Stephen, "You should see him when his body loses its balance. Wandering Aengus I call him" (10.1066). Our immediate supposition is that Stephen's balance is impaired because he drinks too much, but this is merely implied. The language is ambiguous enough to leave room for other explanations. In its early stages, *tabes dorsalis* manifests itself in unsteadiness and staggering. The distinctive tabetic gait usually develops in the later stages.

In "Ithaca" when Bloom and Stephen speculate on the cause of Stephen's earlier "collapse," Bloom thinks of reasons such as drink, drugs, inanition, but Stephen attributes the cause to the "reapparition of a matutinal cloud at first no bigger than a woman's hand" (17.40). Both Bloom and Stephen have earlier seen a cloud that covers the sun. Stephen's allusion is Biblical, referring to the defeat of Ahab by Elijah, which is heralded by "a little cloud out of the sea, like a man's hand" (I Kings 18:44) (Gifford 66). The cloud is an omen of doom for Ahab, the sinner with whom Stephen has earlier identified himself. Significantly, Joyce has changed the quotation to a "*re*apparition" and to a "woman's hand." The first change suggests that Stephen's collapse is related to the *recurrence* of some sign of impending disaster (just as Gogarty's letter indicated that Joyce's gleet was due to a "recurrence of original sin"), the second that his doom is related to woman. Joyce had used the image of the little cloud for the title of one of the stories in *Dubliners*, and he was to use the image again throughout *Finnegans Wake*.[6] The first mention of a cloud in the latter work occurs in a passage that faintly echoes the witches' prophecy in *Macbeth*: "f. t. in Dyfflinarsky ne'er sall fail til heathersmoke and cloudweed Eire's ile sall pall" (13.22), thus conflating the ominous cloud of doom with the image of the weed. Later, the cloud becomes a poisonous cloud, thus doubling its portent of disaster: "Therewith was released in that kingsrick of Humidia a poisoning volume of cloud barrage indeed" (48.4). Clearly, for Joyce, as for Ahab, the image of the cloud foreshadows destruction.

Several characters in the *Wake* also exhibit a peculiarity of gait. Finn MacCool is a "faulterer" and has a "rather strange walk" (131.27, 29), and Shem the Penman has "not a foot to stand on" (169.16). The girl with the kodak had known that Shem "was a bad fast man by his walk on the spot" (172.3). HCE has "tumblerous legs" (88.20) and goes "stambuling haround Dambaling in leaky sneakers," the kind of shoes Joyce frequently wore (33.36). Issy says to Jaunty Jaun, "Coach me how to tumble, Jaime," (461.30). In both the *Scribbledehobble* notebook (33) and the *Wake*, Joyce makes puns on "Jamsey's gait" (258.8; 521.14).

Many of Joyce's friends commented on his strange walk. As early as 1906, Alessandro Francini Bruni observed, "Who could avoid noticing this eccentric during the years that he strolled the streets of Trieste? Agile and lean, his rigid legs like the poles of a compass" (Potts 45), and Silvio Benco admired his "stiff automaton-like bearing" (Potts 52). Two other friends in Trieste, Antonio F. Savio and Lina Galli, described Joyce as "awkward in his gait" (*JJQ* 9: 32, 334). In the 1920s, Nino Frank remembered, "I was struck by the youthful but at the same time uncertain character of Joyce's gait" (Potts 80). Frank Budgen, an artist, was the observer who, upon their first meeting in 1917, captured verbally the most vivid impression of Joyce's aberration: "His walk as he came slowly across to us suggested that of a *wading heron.* The studied deliberateness of a latecomer, I thought at first. But then as he came nearer I saw his heavily glassed eyes and realised that the transition from light interior to darkening garden had made him unsure of a space beset with iron chairs and tables and other obstacles" (emphasis added) (*James Joyce and the Making of Ulysses* 11). The description coincides with that of a tabetic who is deprived of visual cues. Joyce, who read Budgen's book, parodied the above passage in *Finnegans Wake*: "capriole legs covets limbs of a crane" (331.28). In "Calypso" Bloom hastens down the stairs "with a flurried stork's legs" (4.384). During Joyce's later years in Paris, Louis Gillet noted that "To wend his way in the street, he went along tapping the iron point of his white cane on the pavement, with a gesture groping and self-assertive. In fact, this unusual walker was not of this world" (Potts 168). In the late 1930s Jacques Mercanton observed, "He leaned on, or rather seemed to wrap himself around his cane." At other times he described Joyce's "stumbling among the pebbles on the shore," his "undulating walk," his "nimble, rambling gait," and he tells how on more than one occasion he had to grab Joyce's arm to keep him from inadvertently throwing himself against or in front of automobiles (Potts 216, 218, 225, 235, 244).

Joyce's friends seem to have attributed his imbalance to his declining vision, and more than likely poor eyesight did contribute to the problem. Nevertheless, his motor coordination seems to have deteriorated steadily. By 1938, when he performed his customary dance at his birthday party, Nino Frank reports that "Joyce took me by the arms and compelled me to whirl about with him," and that he felt an "agonizing sensation of trying to hold up this man, fragile

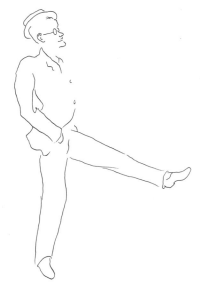

Figure 2. Joyce at Midnight, by Desmond Harmsworth (courtesy of University of Texas at Austin, Harry Ransom Humanities Research Center).

as a statuette" (Potts 94). A year later Joyce wrote to a friend that his birthday festivities of that year would not be accompanied by his famous high-kicking dance (*Ltrs.* III: 436). Whether such a dance could have been performed by someone suffering with *tabes dorsalis* is open to question. However, the disease usually starts insidiously, progresses slowly, and varies in manifestations according to the individual case. (See figure 2.)

In 1921 Joyce made the acquaintance of Dr. Joseph Collins, a neurologist from New York whose avocation was cultivating literary figures. Collins, who earlier had written an article on syphilis for the *American Medical Journal* and a textbook entitled *The Treatment of Nervous Diseases,* would with his trained eye probably have detected and understood the cause of an ataxic gait, if Joyce indeed had one. Collins says that he frequently went on walks with Joyce, though he adds that he never had any professional relations with him (Interviews with Joseph Collins, *Columbia University Oral His-*

tory Collection, Microfiche 18). In his biography of Joyce, Richard Ellmann writes that when Collins read portions of *Ulysses* for the first time, he said that he had in his files writing by insane people as good as this, and he "gave a medical explanation of the deterioration of the artist's brain" (*JJ* 516). Joyce's friend Myron Nutting heard this explanation and wrote about it to Ellmann, but did not specify what it was (*JJ* 790; Ellmann Collection, Tulsa). Collins, in his book *The Doctor Looks at Literature,* devotes an entire chapter to Joyce, mentioning the word "paretic," though not directly in relation to the artist himself (40). In a clever exercise of innuendo, he does say of the author, "Mr. Joyce's ideas of grandeur suggested to a student of psychiatry who heard him talk that he had the mental disease with which that symptom is most constantly associated" (48), delusions of grandeur being one of the early symptoms of paresis. (Because paresis and *tabes dorsalis* both affect the central nervous system, the symptoms sometimes overlap.) Joyce refers to Collins's book in *Finnegans Wake* in regard to the letter from Boston, Mass., which the little hen finds, after which she and her cock had never been "quite their old selves again since that weird weekday in bleak Janiveer . . . when to the shock of both, Biddy Doran looked at literature" (112.25).[7] Collins was published by George Doran Company. Joyce also refers unfavorably to a Dr. Collins in Molly Bloom's soliloquy when she remembers "that dry old stick Dr Collins for womens diseases" (28.1153). In the review of *Ulysses* that Collins wrote for *The New York Times* of 28 May 1922, he calls Joyce's language "base, vulgar, vicious, and depraved," and insinuates that the author was a "potential psychopath." Then he disclaims any "subterfuge on my part to impugn the sanity of Mr. Joyce," whom he calls, "one of the sanest geniuses that I have ever known." (One of the early medical theories about syphilis was that it affected the brain not only adversely, but that "between syphilis and madness there is sometimes room for genius." See Quetel 72.)

Similar, if somewhat less vituperative than Dr. Collins's

remarks, were later reactions to *Finnegans Wake* by Joyce's brother Stanislaus and by Ezra Pound, both of whom also allude to venereal disease in their criticisms. In August of 1924 Stanislaus wrote to Jim: "I don't know whether the drivelling rigmarole about half a tall hat and ladies' modern toilet chambers (practically the only things I understand in this nightmare production) is written with the deliberate intention of pulling the reader's leg or not . . . . perhaps—a sadder supposition—it is the beginning of softening of the brain" (*Ltrs.* III: 103). (*Softening of the brain* is a term that was used at the turn of the century to indicate paresis, which literally did cause a softening of the cortex of the brain. The term occurs in Sir Charles Young's play *Jim the Penman* and also in Ibsen's *Ghosts*.)

Upon reading the book of Shaun, Pound responded similarly: "I will have another go at it, but up to present I make nothing of it whatever. Nothing so far as I make out, nothing short of divine vision or a new *cure for the clapp* can possibly be worth all the circumambient peripherization" (emphasis added) (*Ltrs.* III: 145). Joyce was to echo Pound's phrase in *Finnegans Wake* in his reference to "A New Cure for an old Clap" (104.22).

Pound knew Joseph Collins too and, being intensely interested in Joyce's medical problems, would probably have learned of any medical explanations that Collins ventured of Joyce's condition. In 1926 Pound wrote to Joyce asking him to relay a message to Collins, which Joyce did, through an intermediary (*Pound/Joyce* 225; *Ltrs.* III: 156). Joyce disliked Collins's "pretentious book" and he would have disliked even more Collins's diagnosis being circulated among his friends. One entry of Joyce's *Scribbledehobble* notebook reads, "I suppose he'd like to throw (D. Collins) the 1/2 of them out through the window" (167).

As we have noted with reference to Leopold Bloom, an impaired gait is only the most obvious symptom of *tabes dorsalis*. The other symptoms, which result from damage to nerves that control the sexual organs, bladder, and bowels, and which cause lightning pains and gastric crises, all appear in *Ulysses*, not only in Bloom, but to some degree in Stephen as well, "the son [being] consubstantial with the father" (9.481). Several characters in *Finnegans Wake* exhibit them also. They were, as we have seen, the symptoms from which Joyce himself suffered. "The playwright who wrote the folio of this world . . . is doubtless all in all in all of us" (9.1046).

When in 1904 Oliver Gogarty wrote to his friend Dr. Walsh to ask him to treat Joyce, he jokingly described him as "seeking employment as a waterclock." Joyce was to borrow this figure of speech from Gogarty repeatedly in his later writings. We have already seen Bloom tell Cissy Caffrey that his "waterworks were out of order," punning on clocks in reference to his incontinence. In *Finnegans Wake*, Shem the Penman, who has a "bladder tristended" and a "gush down his fundament" (169.20, 180.23), plans to write a "Ballade Imaginaire which was to be dubbed *Wine, Woman and Waterclocks*" (177.28). The Gripes tells the Mookse, "I am still always having a wish on all my extremeties" (154.15). Finn MacCool is "a horologe unstoppable" (128.1) (Fr. *horloge* meaning clock).

In *Ulysses* Stephen's preoccupation is with waterclosets. Repeatedly he thinks about the death of Arius, fearing the punishment that may be in store for heretics: "Illstarred heresiarch. In a Greek watercloset he breathed his last: euthanasia. With beaded mitre and with crozier, stalled upon his throne . . . with upstiffed omophorion, with clotted hinderparts" (3.51). Likewise in *Finnegans Wake*, HCE "prayed, as he sat on anxious seat . . . during that three and a hellof hours' agony, *ex profundis malorum*" (75.16). In "Circe" Stephen warns the prostitute Zoe to beware "the last end of Arius Heresiarchus. The agony in the closet" (15.2643), and as he leaves the brothel, he asks Bella Cohen, "How much cost?", a question he answers for himself, "Waterloo. Watercloset" (15.3915). In *Finnegans Wake*, in the scene that takes place in the Willingdone Museyroom,

Joyce's choice of imagery indicates that Napoleon meets his Waterloo in a brothel (8-10).[8] *Finnegans Wake* contains numerous references to Waterloo, including one to Finn MacCool as "waterlooged Erin's king" (428.20), and one passage full of cloacal images contains a pun on waterclosets, "the doubleviewed seeds," and on the name of Arius, "Airmienious" (296.1, 8). In the *Wake* the illstarred heresiarch has become "Illstarred punster" (467.29). Joyce too suffered from "the agony in the closet," as we learn from letters he wrote to his brother in 1906 in which he tells, "It is about four or five days since I had the pleasure of defecating," and he complains about the cost of laxatives (*Ltrs.II*: 187, 189).

In *Ulysses* Bloom's interest in sphincters provides a repeated source of humor. In "Hades" he imagines the process of embalming a corpse: "close up all the orifices. Yes, also. With wax. The sphincter loose. Seal up all" (6.425). Later he heads for the National Library to see whether the statues of Hellenic female divinities have anuses. In "Circe" he tells the nymph, "Enemas too, I have administered. One third of a pint of quassia, to which add a tablespoonful of rocksalt. Up the fundament. With Hamilton Long's syringe, the ladies' friend" (15.3397).

Likewise, in "Sirens" Bloom's uncontrollable need to expel gas is very humorous. The problem is not amusing to him, however, causing him great embarrassment: "I must really. Fff. Now if I did that at a banquet" (11.1247). Furthermore, the symptom is recurrent, as indicated by the letter to the editor he imagines writing, beginning "Dear Mr. Editor, what is a good cure for flatulence?" (7.95), and by his purchase of a Wonderworker, "the world's greatest remedy for rectal complaints," to relieve his discomfort (17.1820). One passage of *Finnegans Wake* which contains puns on different gasses (nitrience, exagiants, heliose) includes mention of "the gasbag where the warderworks" (67.9).

In Chapter 2 we noted Bloom's suffering from constipation and incontinence of the bowels. *Finnegans Wake* also contains many references to dung, defecation, and dumps, and many of its characters seem to have problems with incontinence. HCE "admits to having urinated and defecated in the park after the theater, when no public convenience was open" (B. Benstock, *James Joyce* 182). The Norwegian captain is at sea for "Farety days and fearty nights . . . . And the tides made, veer and haul, and the times marred, rear and fall, and holey bucket, dinned he raign!" (312.10). Finn MacCool is pictured sailing away, "Faugh MacHugh O'Bawlar at the wheel . . . ever here and over there, with his fol the dee oll the doo on the flure of his feats and the feels of the fumes in the wakes of his ears our wineman from Barleyhome he just slumped to throne" (382.22). Poor Mark, "the poor old chronometer," is persecuted "because he forgot himself, making wind and water, and made a Neptune's mess of himself" (391.15). Jaun says of HCE, "di'yesmellyspatterygut? . . . Postmartem is the goods" (455.11). Shem the Penman is called "this Calumnious Column of Cloaxity . . . for he seems in a bad bad case" (179.13).

In a review that he wrote of *Portrait of the Artist* in 1917 for the *New Republic* (X 159), H.G. Welles noted Joyce's "cloacal obsession," a remark that rankled enough for Joyce to mock it later in *Ulysses* (7.493). Though Ezra Pound publicly defended Joyce's use of sordid details for artistic purposes, privately he too found Joyce's preoccupation with urination and defecation excessive and tried to encourage him to omit passages which he thought would needlessly offend readers (*Pound/Joyce* 139, 130). Stanislaus Joyce also objected to Joyce's "brooding on the lower order of natural facts" (*Ltrs.* III: 104). Many readers have complained, along with Joyce's beloved Aunt Josephine, that *Ulysses* is unfit to read, to which Joyce countered, hurt and angry, that if *Ulysses* is not fit to read, life is not fit to live (Ellmann, *JJ* 537). My belief is that Joyce's insistence on including so many "natural facts" in his works was based less upon an abstract, naturalistic theory of art to which he adhered, than to a desire to depict the realities of his own existence, albeit in disguise.

Such a preoccupation with physical processes need not be explained in terms of mental abnormality. People in poor health are naturally more concerned with bodily functions than are those whose bodies operate normally.

In "Circe" J.J. O'Molloy defends Bloom against charges of immorality by claiming that his behavior is "due to a momentary aberration of heredity, brought on by hallucination . . . . There have been cases of shipwreck and somnambulism in my client's family . . . . He himself, my lord, is a physical wreck from cobbler's weak chest" (15.945, 953). J.J. O'Molloy's reference to the cobbler points again to the legend of the Wandering Jew, to whom were attributed various occupations, sometimes cobbler, sometimes watercarrier. The reference to weak chest indicates the location of Bloom's "hereditary" illness, just as the location of his bee sting had earlier been identified as "pectoral trauma" (418). Joyce uses here the same excuse for Bloom that he later used for himself, that he is suffering from a hereditary malady. In the *Wake* Shem the Penman is suspected of developing "hereditary pulmonary T. B." (172.13). In Joyce's "Epilogue to Ibsen's *Ghosts*," Captain Alving says, "Reck not to whom the blame is laid,/Y.M.C.A., *V.D.*, T.B." (emphasis added) (Yale, Joyce Collection).

In the summer of 1907, while living in Trieste, Joyce was ill, suffering supposedly from "rheumatic fever." When Oliver Gogarty learned of his illness, he assumed the cause to be less "ethical" than rheumatic fever. In October of that year he wrote to his old friend: "I heard you were stricken with a grievous distemper, and that you were paralyzed. You can understand that the sight of your handwriting rejoiced me, as it disproved the statement that your right arm was paralyzed. I was not a little surprised as well, though the aetiology of a disease which your uncle insisted was altogether ethical should have prepared me for your being miraculously made whole again" (Cornell 540). Clearly Gogarty is alluding to the cyclical nature of Joyce's unethical disease, which would worsen during periods of heightened spirochete activity and then abate during periods of dormancy. Something had happened to Joyce's arm, however, for his brother Charles wrote him asking whether he could use it yet (Cornell 623). In his Trieste diary, Stanislaus wrote on May 23, 1907, that Joyce's right arm was still disabled and that he was receiving "an electric cure" at the Guardia Medica (Ellmann Collection). An entry in one of Joyce's Zurich notebooks is "Trist born with a silver arm up his sleeve . . . paralyzed silver arm" (VI. B. 3, SUNY Buffalo). Ellmann reports that when Joyce consulted a French ophthalmologist in 1922, he attributed his eye problems to "a night's drinking at Pirano in 1910, after which he had spent the early hours of the morning on the ground. This had started arthritic pains in his right shoulder and left the deltoid muscle in his right arm atrophied" (*JJ* 535). Ezra Pound, who took an intense interest in Joyce's health problems, wrote to him in 1917, "Atrophy of the deltoid and biceps shows that the trouble is not necessarily local and confined to the eye" (*Pound/Joyce* 101). Paralysis and subsequent atrophy of muscles can be caused by syphilis, for the formation of tiny lesions in the brain can have effects similar to those of a limited stroke (Interview with Rudolph Kampmeier). In *Finnegans Wake*, Shem the Penman has "one numb arm up a sleeve" and "the wrong shoulder higher than the right" (169.12, 15), and Humphrey Chimpden Earwicker is humpbacked.

Tabes dorsalis sometimes affects the auditory and optic nerves, and thus can cause blindness and in rare cases deafness (Cecil, 7th ed., 402). Hallucinations can also occur; however, these are more likely associated with the use of drugs, or with paresis. As we have noted earlier, because both paresis and *tabes dorsalis* affect the central nervous system, the symptoms sometimes overlap.

Hallucinations occur frequently in *Ulysses*, both in Bloom who is not drunk and in Stephen who is. In the surrealistic "Circe" chapter, both see visions of their past merged with spectres of their suppressed thoughts and feelings.

In his private correspondence, Joyce indicates that he himself had had hallucinatory experiences. In 1917, during the period when he discussed with Pound his medical problems, Pound wrote to him: "About hallucinations. NO medico ever knew anything about the matter. Apply to an alcoholic flagellant in holy orders. Or a vertebraist, as suggested above" (*Pound/Joyce* 100-103). In the 1930s, long after the publication of *Ulysses*, Joyce again suffered from auditory hallucinations (Ellmann, *JJ* 685; *Ltrs.* I: 331-32). In this instance his doctor attributed these experiences to his sudden withdrawal from somniferents.

Tabes dorsalis, as we have seen in regard to Bloom, also causes "lightning" or "lancinating" pains in the extremities, particularly in the feet and legs, and causes "gastric crises," vomiting and sharp pains in the abdominal areas (Cecil, 7th ed. 400-401). Joyce suffered from recurrent gastric problems. As early as February of 1903, he wrote to his father from Paris that he had had a fit of vomiting followed by attacks of neuralgia. Late in 1904, shortly after his elopement with Nora, he wrote to Stanislaus, that he had had a severe cramp in his stomach and that Nora had prayed to God to take his pain away. (In the same letter he bemoans his sight as "lamentable" and says that he needs glasses.[9]) Again, in 1905, "I received your letter today after two days' severe gastrical dissarrangement consequent on your silence." No doubt Joyce enjoyed playing upon people's sympathy or guilt with his complaints, but the nature of the complaints is consistent: "I must break off this letter now as I am not very well. All this trouble and bustle always finds its way into the bosom of my stomach" (*Ltrs.* II: 31, 75, 122, 213). These symptoms continued intermittently throughout the remainder of his life; by the 1930s, the gastric pains had become excruciating. This exacerbation, it turned out was caused by ulcers that eventually perforated and led to peritonitis, which in turn caused his death; his doctors, however, had attributed the pain to "nerves" (Ellmann, *JJ* 665). Dr. Jacques Debray, according to Ellmann's notes, diagnosed

Joyce's trouble as "nervous cramps" (Tulsa). Dr. Thérèse Bertrand-Fontaine described him as having "various mysterious aches and pains" and claimed that he did not have ulcers when she saw him (Tulsa). Paul Leon wrote to Harriet Weaver in April of 1933 describing the intense gastric pain Joyce was suffering and the visit by Dr. Fontaine:

> She came only by six o'clock when the spasmodic attack had passed. She thoroughly examined Mr. Joyce and to our general relief found that there was nothing the matter with him at all. She does not think that he suffers from colitis but on the other attributes the dreadful spasms to a disequilibrium of the system of the sympathetic *nerve* with the *focus* of the dislocation in the epigastric part of his stomach provoking the terrible pains. She . . . declared that the state of his intestines was infinitely better than they were when she last saw them i.e. 3 or 4 years ago. In this part of her diagnostic she in fact confirmed what Dr Debray told me. (*Ltrs. III:* 276-77)

If Joyce's doctors believed that his pain was caused by nerve damage due to *tabes dorsalis,* this would explain why they seem not to have investigated for other physiological causes of his stomach pains. However, they should have been aware that in its advanced stages, *tabes dorsalis* can also cause perforate ulcers (Cecil 7th ed, 402). Shortly after his father's death, Giorgio wrote to Maria Jolas: "If Dr. Fontaine and several other French doctors had been capable of making a proper diagnosis my father would still be alive to-day" (8 Feb. 1941, Maria Jolas Papers, Yale).

By 1907, Joyce's pains no longer confined themselves to the stomach. He complained of "sciatica" of the leg, of rheumatism and neuralgia from that time on. Stanislaus's Trieste diary describes in detail the recurrent bouts of illness which Joyce suffered in those days. The pattern would begin with Jim's increased drinking (probably because he was frightened by impending signs of relapse), then with pains in his back, stomach and sometimes legs, loss of appetite, and excruciating attacks of uveitis, each seemingly worse than the preceding. Stannie describes the rheumatic pains as moving from spot to spot, a characteristic of lightning pains. After a time, the bout would pass and Jim "would miraculously be made whole again," for a while (Trieste diary). In 1916 Nora's uncle, Michael Healy, wrote to him: "I hope you did not knock off carrying the potatoe [sic] in your pocket . . . .Some people put sulphur in their socks as a cure for rheumatism and if you are still troubled with the ailment in your feet perhaps it would be no harm to give it a trial" (Cornell 579).

Bloom, who carries a potato in his pocket, is not the only character in Joyce's works to be described as having "lancinating lightnings." Similar phrases occur in *Finnegans Wake*. "The lightning lancer of Azava Arthur" will accompany the day of judgment, when Finn shall awaken. And Jarl von Hoother goes charging after the prankquean "like the campbells acoming with a fork lance of lightning" (73.36, 22.31).

There is some evidence that not only Bloom but Joyce also suffered from impotence. In October of 1918, while living in Zurich, Joyce met and became enamoured with a woman named Marthe Fleischmann. Like Bloom with his penpal Martha Clifford, Joyce carried on a furtive correspondence and eventually set up a rendezvous with her in Frank Budgen's studio in February of the following year. Bloom contemplates a similar meeting in "Ithaca": "What Possibility suggested itself?/The possibility of exercising virile power of fascination in the not immediate future after an expensive repast in a private apartment in the company of an elegant courtesan, of corporal beauty, moderately mercenary, variously instructed, a lady by origin" (17.1849). After his meeting with Marthe, Joyce told Budgen that he had "explored the hottest and coldest parts of a woman's body," leaving Budgen with the impression that the relationship had not been consummated (Ellmann, *JJ* 451). In

Finnegans Wake is a passage which seems to recount this experience: "old grum has his gel number two (bravevow, our Grum!) and he would like to canoodle her too some part of the time for he is downright fond of his number one but O he's fair smashed on peaches number two so that if he could only canoodle the two, chivee chivoo, all three would feel genuinely happy . . . in his tippy, upindown dippy, tiptoptippy canoodle, can you? Finny [Finis]" (65.20). If the answer to the question "can you?" is negative, as I interpret it to be, this passage would support the supposition of Brenda Maddox that by this time Joyce had become impotent (163). Maria Jolas also confirms this notion: "It is my opinion that at a much earlier age than most men, Joyce left erotic preoccupations, as he did his interest in politics, behind him . . . . Women had ceased to be for him 'the opposite sex,' they were now simply other human beings, neither nobler nor ignobler than men." She attributes his loss of interest in sex to his preoccupation with writing *Finnegans Wake* ("The Joyce I Knew" in *James Joyce: New Perspectives* 184-85).

Impotence is a theme in the *Wake* as well as in *Ulysses*. Shem's riddle, "when is a man not a man?" is answered, "when he is a—yours till the *rending of the rocks*—Sham" [emphasis added] (170.5, 23). HCE in his incarnation as Honuphrius, concupiscent exservicemajor, "instructed his slave Mauritius, to . . . solicit the chastity of [HCE's wife] Anita." Honuphrius has "rendered himself impotent to consummate by subdolence" (572.29-573.22). In the scene in the bedroom of HCE and ALP, his "mace of might" is "mortified" (558.26). As Shari Benstock has observed, "all the sex there is in *Finnegans Wake* (and there's not much really) happened in the past and is rather foggily remembered in the present . . . ; what sex there is in the present is unsuccessful" ("Sexuality and Survival" 186).

Ellmann's biography refers to several conversations between Joyce and various friends, dating to the late 1920s and early 30s, in which Joyce expressed his lack of sexual interest in women and in love-making (631, 639). Brenda Maddox, in her biography of Nora, suggests that the couple's active sexual life ended around 1917 (152). If we consider that at the time Joyce was less than forty years old and that he had been a very sexually active young man, this drastic change in attitude suggests physical alterations beyond the normal process of aging. *Finnegans Wake* contains the cryptic statement, "Pastimes are past times" (263.17).

During the Zurich years, near the time of the Marthe Fleischmann episode, while Joyce was writing *Ulysses*, Frank Budgen and August Suter remember how Joyce encouraged Nora to have affairs with other men. Suter tells of Joyce introducing his wife to Greeks and Jews, "playing with her virtue," and how Nora had "more character and constancy than coquettishness" (Potts 64). Nora told Budgen, "Jim wants me to go with other men so that he will have something to write about" (*Myselves* 188). Both biographers Ellmann and Maddox have accepted Nora's explanation for Joyce's strange behavior, that he was trying to "rehearse a scenario for *Ulysses*" (*Nora* 159), but I believe that Nora, like Molly, either did not understand why her husband was turning from her sexually and encouraging her to have intercourse with other men, or else, more likely, she pretended not to know. Joyce had been wildly jealous in 1909 when he was told that Nora had had sexual relations with Vincent Cosgrave at the same time that he was courting her, and his emotions over her girlhood romance with a young man who died were strong enough to inspire one of his finest stories, "The Dead." It seems unlikely that so possessive a husband, just a few years later, would have wanted her to "go with other men" if he were able to make love with her himself.

In *Finnegans Wake* Joyce recounts the infidelity of the "modern old ancient Irish prisscess" Isolde with the virile young Tristan when she is engaged to marry "poor Mark" who is "shocking poor in his health" (391.25). The princess, who has "nothing under her hat but red hair and solid ivory . . . and a firstclass pair of bedroom eyes," sounds remarkably like Nora (396.7). And the narrator's commentary somewhat resembles Bloom's objective view of Molly's infidelity: "Could you blame her, we're saying, for one psocoldlogical moment? What would Ewe do? With that so tiresome old milkless a ram, with his tiresome duty peck and his bronchial tubes, the tiresome old hairyg orangogran beaver" (396.13).

Joyce's literary preoccupation with the theme of marital infidelity can also be seen in his drama *Exiles*. Here the writer Richard Rowan works half the night in his study and sleeps there too, while his mate Bertha is being seduced by his best friend, Robert Hand. At the end of the play, Richard tells Bertha that he has a "deep, deep wound of doubt in my soul" (*Portable JJ* 626). Again, a hidden wound.

Joyce's attitudes toward women became increasingly hostile as his illness worsened. His remarks, recorded in Stanislaus's Trieste diary, reveal some of these negative feelings: "For us woman is an aperture. We make no difference between a whore and a wife except that a whore we have for five minutes, a wife all our life" (7 April 1907). A year later, Stannie wrote, "Jim's dislike for women has grown almost savage" (Tulsa). That his negativity did not abate with time can be seen in the 14 November 1930, entry of Stuart Gilbert's Paris journal: "JJ drank well and was expansive. Believes in long dresses for women: anti-feminist. 'La femme c'est rien' is one of his remarks" (*Reflections on James Joyce* 34).

It would be understandable (even if not reasonable) for a man suffering the consequences of a venereal infection to blame woman as the cause of his disease. Repeatedly in *Ulysses*, either through Bloom or through Stephen, Joyce expresses this idea. As he wrote to Harriet Weaver in March of 1924, woman is like the river Anna Liffey: "Her Pandora's box contains the ills flesh is heir to. The stream is quite brown, rich in salmon, very devious, shallow." Then later he adds, almost apologetically, "All

Pandora's gifts are not maladies" (*Ltrs.* I: 213). At the opening of *Ulysses,* Stephen's feelings toward women have
changed from the ecstasy that he felt at the end of *Portrait
of the Artist* to a fear of contamination. He looks at the old
milk woman and imagines her "woman's unclean loins . . .
the serpent's prey" (1.421). He characterizes the
cocklepickers as "the ruffian and his strolling mort," imagining the woman a whore by night, "A shefiend, whiteness
under her rancid rags" (3.372, 379). When Mr. Deasy, whose
wife had left him, voices his prejudices against women, de-
claring that woman brought sin into the world, Eve, Helen
of Troy, MacMorrough's wife who, he believed, had first
brought the strangers to Irish shores, Parnell's mistress,
Stephen remains mute. Although he had contested Deasy's
bigoted opinions about Jews, their views on women seem
more compatible, for Stephen echoes similar notions in
"Proteus," thinking of Eve as "Womb of sin" (3.44); in
"Nestor" he remembers that Pyrrhus had "fallen by a
beldam's hand" (2.48); and in "Scylla and Charybdis" he
notes that "if the shrew is worsted yet there remains to her
woman's invisible weapon" (9.460). The ballad of the Jew's
daughter who murders little Harry Hughes, the song that
Stephen tactlessly sings to Bloom in "Ithaca," reflects as
much his fear of castrating women as his prejudice against
Jews, the former being what Stephen may have intended,
while Bloom heard the latter:

> She took a penknife out of her pocket
> And cut off his little head
> And now he'll play his ball no more
> For he lies among the dead.
>   [17.825]

On the surface, Bloom's attitude toward women seems
more affectionate, more considerate and sympathetic, than
Stephen's, as evidenced by his concern for Mrs. Breen and
Mrs. Purefoy. However, Bloom also has repressed fears and
hostilities toward the female sex. In his conscious thoughts,

he attributes the invention of barbed wire to a nun, and he observes the cruel glances that more fortunate women cast at Mrs. Breen. At an unconscious level, he associates his wife with the pet cat: both are demanding, self-centered, and cruel. Only in his fantasies in "Circe" does Bloom fully reveal his unconscious antagonisms toward the opposite sex. There Bloom's Boys sing:

> The wren, the wren,
> The king of all birds,
> Saint Stephen's his day
> Was caught in the furze [bush].
> [15.1451]

(In the *Wake* this chant becomes "The Fenn, the Fenn, the kinn of all Fenns!" [376.33].) The fan reminds Bloom that in his home, "the missus is master. Petticoat government" (15.2759); and the nymph threatens him with castration, "You'll sing no more lovesongs" (15.3459). Bloom's confrontation with Bella Cohen and his consequent transformation into a woman reveal his fear of total emasculation. In his fantasies, Molly bears a resemblance to Bella, the castrating female. In "Circe" both women berate him for keeping them "waiting" when he fails to "come."

We have already made note of Bloom's mental association of prostitutes with venereal infection. At his first opportunity he warns Stephen: "he spoke a word of caution *re* the dangers of nighttown, women of ill fame and swell mobsmen, which barely permissible once in a while though not as a habitual practice, was of the nature of a regular deathtrap for young fellows of his age" (16.63). Bloom wants brothels to be made safer. While wondering what to do with "our wives," he considers the possibility of "masculine brothels, state inspected and medically controlled" (17.668).

Finnegans Wake also contains many allusions to women, especially to prostitutes, as a source of infection. We have already seen that Shem is "prost bitten," and that Finn tumbles because of the "bitch bite at his ear." The union of "a fammished devil" and "a young *source*ress" (emphasis added) leads to "eternal conjunction," though in this case the young sorceress is as likely the victim as the perpetrator, for the young man (in this scene Glugg) is "having that pecuniarity ailmint . . . because souffrant chronic from a plenitude of house torts" (251.12, 241.5). Later we hear "May St. Jerome of the Harlots' Curse make family three of you which is much abedder!" (252.11), suggesting the infection of the female and offspring by the male.

Joyce uses many recurrent motifs in *Ulysses* to suggest the physical destruction that has occurred to Bloom and Stephen, one of the more prominent being, as we have noted earlier, the image of the shipwrecked sailor, a conflation of Gogarty's Sindbad, Dante's Ulysses, and the crew of Christopher Columbus. In "Eumaeus" Stephen sings two songs about shipwreck, *Youth here has End* and *Johannes Jeep* (J.J.), "about the clear sea and the voices of the sirens, sweet murderers of men" (16.1813). As we have noted earlier, references to shipwreck continue in the *Wake*, Joyce's imagery echoing Gogarty's poem on Sindbad (275.18; 155.9; 378.10).

But the primary metaphor for physical destruction in Joyce's autobiographical fictions, beginning with *Dubliners* and recurring through all his novels, is that of the Fall. Though symbolically this image suggests spiritual decline, Joyce's use of it always emphasizes the physical consequences of falling. For example, the story "Grace" opens with drunken Tom Kernan fallen at the bottom of stairs, lying in "filth and ooze" in the restroom of a Dublin pub, his mouth bloody because he has bitten off the tip of his tongue as a result of his fall. In *Portrait of the Artist* also, as we have seen, Stephen suffers physical illness when he falls. This motif is repeated in *Ulysses* when Bloom recalls his experience with Lotty Clarke, high on Ben Howth, in terms of a fatal fall: "Thirty-two head over heels per second. Press nightmare. Giddy Elijah. Fall from cliff. Sad end of government printer's clerk" (15.3374). Later he points to his hand which bears a scar: "That weal there is an accident. Fell and cut it twenty-two years ago. I was sixteen" (15.3713). According to Ellmann's account, based upon Stanislaus's Trieste diary, Joyce was about fourteen when he had his first sexual experience, but an unpublished letter from Joyce to Paul Leon, quoted by Ellmann, indicates that he might have been sixteen (*JJ* 47, 658n). Drunken Stephen says that he too hurt his hand falling off his hobbyhorse sixteen years ago. At that time, Bloom would have been the same age that Stephen is now, twenty-two. In 1904, when he was first treated for venereal disease, Joyce was twenty-two years old. Thus it would seem that the fall of Stephen/Bloom/Joyce has caused the scar of Ulysses.[10]

In *Finnegans Wake*, the image of the Fall assumes mythic proportions, accompanied by a recurrent clap of applause, or a clap of thunder. "Clappyclapclap" in *Ulysses* becomes "klikkaklakkaklaskaklopatzklatschabattacreppycrottygraddaghsemmih sammihnouithappluddyappladdypkonpkot!" in the *Wake* (44.20). This crash is made up of the sound of the word *clap* in many different languages. Other recurrent crashes are made up of the word *thunder* (McHugh, *Annotations* 1, 23). The first word suggests the occurrence of venereal disasters; the second, fear of God's retribution. In the *Wake*, each time a character falls, he is transformed into a lower form of life: from Finn to Earwicker to Shem; from Shaun to Jaun to Yawn. These cyclical transformations suggest physiological deterioration. In the cycles of syphilis, each recurrence is more virulent than the preceding one.

Joyce was deathly afraid of thunder, which he identified with the wrath of God and with disaster. In a handwritten memoir entitled "Souvenirs de voyage" (c. 1930), Stuart Gilbert describes Joyce's reaction to a loud clap of thunder when they travelled together through the Alps by train: "I saw his face grow pale and his long fingers twitching nervously. It was not fear in the ordinary sense of the word he felt but an almost religious awe, as if God had spoken" (U. of Texas, Gilbert Collection). In *Ulysses*, Stephen, Bloom, and Molly all hear the thunder; Molly Bloom describes its significance: "that thunder woke me up God be merciful to us I thought the heavens were coming down about us to punish us" (18.134).

In "The Ballad of Finnegans Wake," Tim Finnegan, the drunken hod-carrier who falls off a ladder to his demise is a corruption of Finn MacCool, the great legendary hero of Ireland, who also falls in battle with his enemies. Joyce conflates the thunderous fall of Tim Finnegan from his ladder with many other fatal falls: with that of Ibsen's *Masterbuilder*, who at the instigation of a woman climbs the edifice he has constructed and then falls to his death; with the fall of Napoleon at Waterloo; with the fall of Brian Boru at Clontarf; with the fall of Charles Parnell; with the fall of Humpty Dumpty. The common thread is that as a result of the Fall, the man is physically broken beyond repair. O felix culpa! So end Finn MacCool and all his reincarnations. "O foenix culprit! "(*FW* 23.16).

In *Finnegans Wake* the sleeping twins, Kevin and Jerry Jehu (J.J.), are "so tightly tatached [Fr. *tache* meaning spot or stain] as two maggots to touch other." The narrator's comment is "O, foetal sleep! Ah, fatal slip!" (562.21; 563.10). We have seen in *Portrait* that the word FOETUS carved on a medical school desk caused Stephen to have "monstrous reveries," and that in *Ulysses* Bloom is overwhelmed with guilt over the death of his newborn son, Rudy. Also, we recall, Joyce minutely inspected the foetus of the child that Nora miscarried in 1908. In the *Wake* the concern over the children, particularly the daughter, continues: "now godsun shine on menday's daughter; a good clap, a fore marriage, a bad wake, tell hell's well" (117.4).

James and Nora Joyce eloped in October of 1904 and their children were born in July of 1905 and July of 1907, both within less than three years of their parents' union. A year later, Nora miscarried a third child after taking a pre-

scribed "arsenical medicine," a medication probably intended to treat her infection and that of her unborn child
(Trieste diary of Stanislaus, Tulsa). The more recently a
mother is infected with syphilis, the greater the likelihood
her children will be affected (Kampmeier, "Late and Congenital Syphilis" 36-37). Also, should she become pregnant
shortly after infection, the less likely that she herself will
have severe symptoms of the disease, for her own resistance
to it will be stronger. Three out of four women with untreated syphilis of less than two years' duration will give
birth to a syphilitic stillborn or living infant (Cecil, 7th ed.,
383). As we have noted, however, not every child of an infected mother will be affected, even if she is in the early
stages of infection. If the mother's disease is of more than
four years' duration and has become latent, she may at that
point be able to bear normal children. Furthermore, an infected child will not necessarily show obvious signs of infection at birth, or even for years afterwards. If the spirochetes are present only in the nervous system, the symptoms may not become apparent until adolescence or young
adulthood.

Around 1929, at the age of twenty-two, Lucia Joyce
began to show indications of physical deterioration, and in
the early 1930s her behavior became increasingly abnormal. According to her father, doctors attributed her condition to schizophrenia, but if Joyce was indeed suffering from
syphilis when he eloped with her mother in 1904, it is also
possible that Lucia's madness was a result of paresis, which
can be transmitted *in utero.*

Exactly when Lucia's mind became affected is difficult
to determine. One touching letter from Nora to her sister-
in-law Eileen, written when Lucia was five, depicts a happy
little girl: "we say good night to Lucia and she goes up to
bed singing she is wonderful" (*Ltrs.* II: 302). Joyce alludes
to Lucia's impending illness in *Finnegans Wake* by noting
the little cloud, followed by "Singabed sulks before slumber" (256.33-34). A lengthy account of her medical case
history, written in French by Joyce and Paul Leon in 1934,

indicates that in early childhood she was extremely cheerful, but that problems began after she turned five or six. Dr. Thérèse Bertrand-Fontaine, who treated Joyce in Paris, told Richard Ellmann that "Lucia showed signs of dementia when she was fifteen or sixteen." Valery Larbaud, in an interview with Ellmann, places the age at which he found her "strange" at fourteen. However, Myron Nutting, who knew the family around 1925, found Lucia "the most normal" of them all. Samuel Beckett's comment was that, "Lucia, even before her breakdown, would sometimes come to dinner, not eat much, disappear, and vomit. Otherwise she appeared normal" (Ellmann Collection, Tulsa). Ellmann took notes during Lucie Leon's account of what she claimed was the first day that Lucia went really mad: "She had come over to her apartment feeling rather ill and had asked her to give her something to do, anything, something to sew or knit . . . .suddenly the girl collapsed and seemed to be about ready to faint. When she was put on the bed and revived a little, she began to rebel against everything, *attacked everyone* . . . . Mme. Leon . . . thought it was a *latent condition* not brought on by any specific cause" (emphasis added) (Tulsa). Certainly the circumstances of Lucia's life (being moved from one country to another, being isolated from young people her own age, having no successful love life, being the daughter of a famous author) could all account for mental problems. Joyce's case history offers many plausible reasons for her illness and indicates that her condition had been diagnosed as schizophrenia "avec des element[s] pithiatique." However, he also says, in the report written for doctors of the sanitorium to which he was transferring her, that she was certain that she suffered from tuberculosis, from leprosy, from syphilis.

Many of Lucia's behavioral symptoms, poor judgment, increased libido, personality change, memory loss, illusions of grandeur, paranoia, catatonic seizures, fatigue, neglect of personal appearance and body cleanliness, deteriorating handwriting, restlessness, inability to sleep, loss of appetite, all point to the possibility of *either* paresis *or* schizophrenia

(Cecil, 7th ed. 404-5; *American Handbook of Psychiatry*, Vol. 3, "Schizophrenia: The Manifest Symptomatology" 524-47, and Vol. 4, "Neurosyphilitic Conditions: General Paralysis, General Paresis, Dementia Paralytica" 134-49 ; *Modern Psychiatry* 458-78; 535-51). Because the symptoms of either disease differ with each individual case, and because they can so much resemble each other, the only sure way to distinguish paresis from schizophrenia is through laboratory tests, which in the past were not infallibly accurate. As of 1975, the Wassermann and Kahn blood tests were positive in 95 percent of paresis cases. Tests of the spinal fluid of an *untreated* paretic patient almost invariably indicated a positive Wassermann. This would not necessarily hold true if the patient had been previously treated. Letters of Joyce to Giorgio and to Frank Budgen claim that Lucia was tested for syphilis, with negative results, but his letters do not tell the precise nature of the tests nor exactly when they were administered.

Some of Lucia's symptoms, increased libido, bold sexual overtures, and outbursts of violence, particularly the latter, are more closely identified with the symptoms of paresis than with schizophrenia. Descriptions of Lucia's behavior as described in detail by friends and by Brenda Maddox in her biography *Nora* match closely textbook descriptions of paresis: "The most important motor disturbances are convulsions and apoplectic phenomena. They appear in any stage of the disease and are present in 35-65 percent of cases. Psycho-motor attacks or epileptic equivalents occur, manifested by sudden periods of excitement, *extreme violence*, and impulsive shouting . . . . In successfully treated patients, the convulsions, as a rule, cease entirely" (*American Handbook of Psychiatry*, Vol. 4, 141). Another authority describes the illness thus:

> the intitial manifestations have to do with an insidious change of character, a progressive failing of mentality, deterioration of personality, and diminution of physical health. . . . . Because the cortical influence is diminished by

the disease, there is a decreased control over the feeling of irritability or pleasure. Thus the slightest disturbance which in the normal person might create a fleeting, hardly noticeable resentment will result in a violent emotional outburst by the patient; conversely, the slightest flattery, attention, or wit which appeals to the patient will create uproarious laughter. For this same reason, whatever [s]he wants, whether sex satisfaction, food, alcohol, or approval of others, [s]he will attempt to obtain in the most direct fashion—regardless of the conventions. (Sadler 538-39)

We have already noted Lucie Leon's description of Lucia's first attack of "madness," indicating the violent nature of her actions. In other instances, Joyce wrote Harriet Shaw Weaver that Lucia "boxes the nurses" (Ltr. of 21 Oct.1932, Tulsa), and to Carola Giedion-Welcker that she was kept under close surveillance (*Ltrs* III, 323). According to Maddox, Lucia not only struck her mother but also threw a chair at her, and later, after attacking patients and nurses, had to be confined in a straitjacket (278-79). In the Ellmann papers is a statement by Dr. Pierre Leulilier, director of the Clinic of the Villa Les Pays, dated 25 April 1936, saying that Lucia needed to be moved to another institution because she was "dangerous" (Tulsa).

Schizophrenics lack the ability to relate to other people. Yet Joyce insisted that "The only hold she seems to have on life is her affection for us" (Sept. 1934, *Ltrs* III, 323). After her hospitalization in Zurich, Joyce found it necessary to appease Lucia's desire to have her parents nearby, so that when he took a holiday, he would go to elaborate pains to prevent her knowing how far he and Nora had travelled (correspondence with Stuart Gilbert, U. of Texas). Lucia's deep dependency upon and attachment to her parents does not sound like the withdrawal of schizophrenia.

Despite many behavioral similarities in the two illnesses, paresis and schizophrenia are very different in nature. Schizophrenia is a mental condition, a retreat from reality triggered by environmental circumstances, a disruption of personality, of sensory perceptions and of thought processes, due to a chemical imbalance in the body. (The biochemical aspects are fairly recent discoveries. They are described in later literature, but not in *Modern Psychiatry*, published in 1945.) Unlike paresis, which is an invasion of the brain and spinal tissue by the spirochete *Trepona pallidum*, schizophrenia is not an infection.

Paresis creates physical changes as well as mental ones, especially an overall weakening of the entire muscular system which, if the disease goes untreated, leads eventually to paralysis. Before showing obvious signs of personality disorder, Lucia gave up her dancing career because she said she was too weak to continue. Another of the symptoms of paresis is a change in facial expression: "The face becomes expressionless and devoid of normal mimic motions. There is flattening and smoothing out of the nasolabial folds" (*American Handbook of Psychiatry*, Vol. 4, 141). Photographs of Lucia in her youth do seem strongly lacking in expression. I do not wish to insist here that Lucia certainly was infected with paresis, only to indicate that some of her symptoms do point to that possibility.

In 1934, when Lucia was institutionalized at Kusnacht, a young woman doctor, a student of Carl Jung's, visited her there. Years later, the doctor's daughter, Ximena de Angulo Roelli, provided Richard Ellmann with a copy of her mother's notes on Lucia taken at the time. She reported that her "walk is distressing—she shuffles along like an old woman, and is stooped far forward." (Contracture of neck muscles is one symptom of paresis.) Again, this description seems to point to a physical ailment rather than a purely mental one. Lucia told the young woman that she didn't think Jung could do anything for her, "because my trouble is somewhere in the body." She inquired about her high leucocyte count, and when told that white blood cells provided the body with defenses against the invasion of microbes, she pointed to her head and said they should go up there. Again, the high count of white blood cells (as well as other unspecified anomalies of her blood found by Dr.

Naegeli, one of the foremost experts in Europe; see *Ltrs.* I, 357) points to a physical cause of her illness. When Joyce came to visit her in the sanitorium, she told him in the young woman doctor's hearing, "not to pretend that he did not know what was the matter with her . . . . that she had syphilis. She explained to him that he was not to think she thought she had inherited it from him—it was her own fault that she had it" (Ellmann Collection, Tulsa).

In June of 1934, according to Joyce's case history, Lucia was administered "fever treatment, against which she is violently opposed, but she seemed to be clearer in her ideas during her fever."[11] On June 1, 1934, Joyce wrote to Giorgio, "They called in a German specialist at Nyon and he advised them to treat Lucia as if she had something or other, though there is no trace of it. And this apparently is doing her good" (Ellmann, *JJ* 673). In 1917, before the advent of penicillin, doctors had discovered that to infect victims of paresis with malaria fever helped and sometimes cured them. Raising the body temperature killed the spirochetes in the spinal fluid which were impervious to arsenical treatment. At first the patients were deliberately infected with malaria, but eventually forms of artificially induced fever were devised to produce the same results. In one of these, the person was placed in a box resembling a coffin and heated to within a degree or two of death. If this treatment seems extreme today, we must consider that up to this time, paresis victims had a 100 percent mortality rate, and that after the introduction of fever treatment, "40% of the parctics recovered sufficiently to lead useful lives. Many recovered completely" (Parran 19). According to Dr. Hansruedi Isler, neurologist, Lucia's treatment, *pyrifère*, or in German *Pyriferkur*, was "indeed the successor of Wagner von Jauregg's famous malaria fever cure for paresis, using the so-called pyrogen substances (bacterial proteins causing fever on injection) to induce fever as a treatment for general paresis of the insane" (Ltr. of 10 February 1993). Treatment for the condition, Dr. Isler points out, cannot be equated with a positive diagnosis of paresis. Nevertheless, it does provide one more in-

stance of syphilis being "suspected" by doctors as the cause
of a Joycean malady. Also, the fact that Lucia seemed
"clearer in her thoughts" during her fever suggests that the
treatment may have had beneficial effects. If nerve damage from paresis were extensive, however, fever treatment
could not cure symptoms, only halt the progress of the disease. Partially recovered patients are described thus:

> In some cases the premorbid intellectual and emotional sta-
> tus cannot be restored. These patients require permanent
> institutional care . . . .In most of these patients, the delu-
> sions and the bizarre behavior have disappeared; they now
> represent all stages of mental deterioration. In some in-
> stances, cyclothymic manifestations have come into promi-
> nence, and others exhibit a schizophrenic picture with man-
> nerism and oddities which in no way can be differentiated
> from the classical type of schizophrenia. Since in some of
> these cases the spinal fluid abnormalities have reverted to
> normal and the pupillary reactions also have become nor-
> mal, there are no longer clinical signs in the conventional
> sense of an organic psychosis . . . .Patients with residual
> brain damage at times have periods of acute agitation and
> require treatment with tranquilizing drugs. (*American Hand-
> book of Psychiatry*, Vol. 4, 146)[12]

With untreated paresis Lucia would not have lived as long
as she did, until 1982 to the age of seventy-five, but because she was given fever treatment, paresis cannot be excluded as a possible cause of her madness on the grounds
that she lived too long.

Also in 1934, after his daughter had exhibited signs of
insanity, Joyce wrote a parodic poem entitled "Epilogue to
Ibsen's 'Ghosts'" (a drama in which Captain Alving trans-
mits syphilis to his son but not to his illegitimate daughter).
Joyce's poem asks why this should happen:

> Both swear I am the self-same man
> By whom their infants were begotten.

Explain, fate, if you care or can
Why one is sound and one is rotten.
                              (*JJ* 670)

The answer to the riddle, as Dr. J.B. Lyons has noted, is that the syphilitic father was more recently infected (hence more contagious) when he sired the first child. By the time the second child was conceived, his disease had become latent and he did not infect the second mother (*James Joyce and Medicine* 89). When Herman Gorman quoted from this poem in his biography of Joyce, the author objected to his placing it so near the account of Lucia's illness, saying that to do so caused it to appear "almost biographical" (Ellmann Collection, Tulsa).

Arthur Power recalls, "For Joyce, for whom Creation, Origin, and Paternity were the secret of being, no tragedy could have gone deeper [than the illness of Lucia] and the image of his sick child tortured him, for with his peculiar theories of paternity he considered himself as the father, the guilty source" (*The Joyce We Knew* 116).

Like Molly Bloom, in 1909 Nora Joyce was troubled by a "brown stain" on her drawers about which her husband commented frequently (*SL* 184, 185, 189). Brenda Maddox, Nora's biographer, states that "Nora is known to have suffered from gynecological difficulties," and she interprets a cryptic remark, "still continues," in one of Nora's undated letters to Joyce, written when their children were very young, as a "husband-wife code for some kind of vaginal discharge" (113). *Finnegans Wake* contains several references to dirty drawers. ALP collects spoiled goods in her knapsack, among them "brooches [breeches] with bloodstaned breeks in em . . . midgers and maggets, ills and ells . . . and pleures of bells" [Fr. *pleurer* meaning to weep], the passage ending, "Undo lives' end. Slain." (11.21-28). Another reference linking illness to panties occurs in the following passage: "ana *mala* woe is we! A pair of *syco*panties with amygdaleine eyes" (emphasis added) (94.15). HCE, who calls ALP "Fulvia Fluvia," recalls how he "waged love on her: and *spoiled her undines*. And she wept: O my lors!" (emphasis added) (547.7-8). ALP, in a passage which I shall discuss later, refers to herself as "the pantymammy" (626.27).

Nora Joyce also had many physical complaints which she attributed to "nerves." In 1917 she took her two children to Locarno for a rest, and while she was there she wrote to her husband that her hair continued to fall out very much and mentioned how nervous she was (Cornell 758). (Alopecia, or falling hair, is a symptom of secondary syphilis.) In *Finnegans Wake* is a reference to Nora's hair loss: "First she let her hair fal and down it flussed to her feet its teviots winding coils" (206.29). Apparently Joyce was concerned enough to telephone her, and in her next letter she reassured him that she was a little better. Shortly thereafter, in Zurich, Joyce suffered a severe eye attack which necessitated surgery, and Nora rushed to his side. However she must have continued to feel unwell: before the couple left Zurich to return to Trieste in 1919, she went to see a doctor, a specialist in internal medicine and a cardiologist (Maddox 167).

Years later, in November of 1928, Nora was hospitalized for minor surgery and given radium treatments. Shortly afterwards she underwent a hysterectomy. (Venereal infections increase the likelihood of cervical cancer.) Joyce repeatedly told friends and relatives that she had cancer, and the account of Nora's illness given to Ellmann by Helen Joyce, Giorgio's wife, confirms what Joyce said about radium treatments, the use of which, prior to surgery, was the standard procedure for cervical cancer in the 1920s (Interview with Rudolph Kampmeier). It is ironic, however, that Joyce should have had Molly suggest some seven years earlier that she might have "something growing" inside her.

Just a few months before Nora's surgery, Joyce himself had developed a "large boil" on his right shoulder after which his doctors gave him three-weeks' series of injections of arsenic, followed by treatments of "iodine" (*Ltrs.* I: 266, 270, 280). Iodides were the recommended treatment at that time for gummata of tertiary syphilis, which, when they occurred on the skin, resembled large ulcers. In *Finnegans Wake* one of the drinkers in the tavern says, "the kersse of my armsore appal this most unmentionablest of men" (320.12). And at the wake, one of the mourners says to Finn, "so may the priest of seven worms and scalding tay*boil,* Papa Vestray, come never anear you" (26.6). If Joyce had not told his doctors in Paris that he had been infected with syphilis as a young man, and they had reason for the first time in 1928 to believe that he was syphilitic, they would probably have insisted upon checking his wife, for syphilis is almost always a family disease. There is no indication whether they checked his children.

As early as 1904, Joyce began to be bothered by his eyesight. He wrote in Stanislaus in December, "I shall go to an oculist next month to get pincenez glasses which I can use on occasions as my sight is lamentable." Two years later, in December of 1906, he again complained of his eyes. Within a few months he was suffering with his first severe bout of uveitis and with "rheumatic fever." Because it can also be caused by many other diseases or infections, iritis (or uveitis) cannot in itself be considered evidence of syphilis; nevertheless, acquired syphilis was one of the leading causes of this eye ailment, more so during Joyce's lifetime than at present, because the incidence of advanced syphilitic complications was much greater before the advent of penicillin (see medical sources quoted in Prologue of this work). Furthermore, the fact that by 1932 Joyce's retina and optic nerve were also involved, that the uveitis was posterior rather than anterior, points to syphilis as a likely cause of his problems (Duke-Elder 545-46, 228).

Both uveitis and relapse of secondary symptoms are more likely to appear in a syphilitic patient if he has been inadequately treated in the early stages of the disease (Cecil,

7th ed., 366, 360). Even in the days of arsenical treatment, which was much more effective than mercury, months of chemical therapy were required to cure syphilis, and then the outcome was uncertain. In the early stages of his illness, Joyce had, at best, been treated with mercury in 1904. Arsenic did not become the preferred treatment until 1909. Yet without any treatment, or with inadequate treatment, symptoms will disappear in the natural progress of the disease. In 1907, a few months before his daughter was born, Joyce suffered an illness which could have been a relapse of syphilis, and it was at this time that he first developed severe uveitis. It seems at least possible that he was one of those inadequately treated patients who later developed uveitis and suffered relapse, or perhaps the eye complications signaled the beginning of the tertiary phase of the disease. (In either case, he would probably have been more contagious during the period of increased spirochete activity than earlier.)

Gonorrhea can also cause uveitis, but gonococcal uveitis tends to be less severe than that which is caused by syphilis (Interview with Dr. Harold Akin, ophthalmologist). Joyce repeatedly called his disease "rheumatic iritis," a term which was used to refer to gonococcal uveitis. As we have noted, a letter to Richard Ellmann from Dr. Pierre Merigot de Treigny, who saw Joyce in Paris, says that Joyce suffered from "rheumatical iritis" (Tulsa). Rheumatic iritis is *not* a symptom of rheumatic fever (Berens, *The Eye and Its Diseases* 822).

Another condition of the eyes caused by syphilis is the Argyll-Robertson pupil associated with neurosyphilis, particularly with *tabes dorsalis.* The pupils become fixed, often closed to just a pinprick opening, and fail to adjust to light but do react to accommodation. Occasionally they are enlarged (Cecil, 7th ed. 402). The first surgery performed on Joyce's eyes, an iridectomy, was to remove bits of the iris to enlarge the pupil (Ellmann, *JJ* 412, 417). In *Ulysses* the insect-like grandfather Virag declares to Bloom, "You shall find that these night insects follow the light. An illusion for remember their complex unadjustable eye" (15.2421). And Bloom uses a stuffed owl to explain to Milly "certain abnormalities of vision" (17.912).

In 1916 Joyce, who had for some years corresponded with Ezra Pound but had not yet met him in person, sent Pound a photograph of himself. Pound wrote back that he found the appearance of Joyce's eyes "a bit terrifying" and questioned him regarding his doctors' opinions and prescriptions (*Pound/Joyce* 85). Years later Joyce told Harriet Weaver that Pound had been able to tell from a photograph the pathological condition of his eyes (*SL* 248). The time at which Pound saw the picture was before Joyce's eye problems had become so severe as to require surgery, after which one of his eyes appeared cloudy. Possibly whatever Pound saw had to do with the appearance of Joyce's pupils.

In *Ulysses* both Bloom and Stephen have relatively mild problems with their eyes. Stephen, unlike young Joyce, had worn glasses since his childhood. In "Lotus-Eaters" Bloom watches a stylish woman getting into a cab, "Drawing back his head and gazing far from beneath his veiled eyelids he saw the bright fawn skin shine in the glare, the braided drums," and he thinks, "Clearly I can see today. Moisture about gives long sight perhaps" (5.112). Not long afterwards, however, in "Lestrygonians," he thinks, "Must get those old glasses of mine set right. Goerz lenses, six guineas." His eyes fail him when he tries to read a distant clock:

> There's a little watch up there on the roof of the bank to test those glasses by.
> His lids came down on the lower rims of his irides. Can't see it. If you imagine it's there you can almost see it. Can't see it. (8.554-63)

Stephen's experiences are similar. We have already noted his fear of blindness. In "Proteus" he thinks, "Flat I see, then think distance, near, far, flat I see, east, back. Ah, see now. Falls back suddenly, frozen in stereoscope. Click does the trick" (3.418). In "Circe" when he pays Bella Cohen, he gives her too much money, saying, "my sight is somewhat troubled" (15.3546). Later, looking at a match, he says, "Lynx eye. Must get glasses. Broke them yesterday. Sixteen years ago. Distance. The eye sees all flat" (15.3628).

Bloom's eyes seem to have some abnormal appearance which other people notice, for at various times in the novel, characters refer to him as "dark eyes," "pale Galilean eyes," "cod's eye," "plumeyes," "old sloppy eyes," and "white-eyed kafir," the latter suggesting iris atrophy. The eye imagery so recurrent in "Cyclops" seems to point to another of Bloom's symptoms.

In *Finnegans Wake* eye problems are more severe: "When Phishlin Phil wants throws his lip 'tis pholly to be fortune flonting and whoever's gone to mix Hotel by the salt say water there's nix to nothing we can do for he's never again to sea [see]" (50.33).

Stephen Dedalus's concerns about his vision are emphasized in "Circe," when he sees the apparition of Edward the Seventh, the supposedly poxy prince (the "peacemaker") wearing the halo of Joking Jesus (J.J.), and reciting part of Mulligan's ballad: "My methods are new and are causing surprise. To make the blind see I throw dust in their eyes" (15.4478). Sand [spirochetes] from the Red Sea [blood] has caused the sailor in "Eumaeus" to become "bad in the eyes" (16.1674). Stephen's fear is that God will punish him with blindness, fear which may stem from an incident in his childhood when the fanatically religious Mrs. Riordan (Dante) told him that if he didn't apologize, the eagles would come and pull out his eyes (*Portrait* 8). The notion that blindness is God's punishment to the sinner is repeated when the blind stripling says to Cashel Boyle O'Connor Fitzmaurice Tisdall Farrell, "God's curse on you, whoever you are! You're blinder nor I am, you bitch's bastard!" (10.1119). Bloom echoes this phrase later in "Sirens" when the barmaids mention the blind piano tuner: "God's curse on bitch's bastard" (11.285). "God's curse" is another name that was given to syphilis, a curse that can account for the blindness of the stripling, for the dementia of Cashel, and for the misfortunes of the bitch's bastard. Variations of the same phrase echo through the *Wake* as "Gall's curse," "Gog's curse," "Goth's scourge," and "ditcher's dastard" (46.15; 73.6; 251.2; 586.15).

By thus tracing the physiological references in *Ulysses*, along with some of those in *Finnegans Wake*, we see that the lower side of Joyce's puns and allusions lead us back to the mythic themes of guilt, sin, and retribution that we examined in the preceding chapter. God's punishment for sexual sins, according to traditional belief, is venereal disease. That Joyce accepted this correlation between sin and punishment is made clear in one cryptic entry of his *Scribbledehobble* notebook, another pun:

Cock's ill = God's will (26).

4

An Insectfable

Upon learning of Joyce's infection with venereal disease, Oliver Gogarty wrote to him, "Well the canker has attacked Art," thus providing Joyce with another important metaphor for his work. In *A Portrait of the Artist As a Young Man*, Stephen Dedalus memorizes the sentences in his spelling books:

> Wolsey died in Leicester Abbey
> Where the abbots buried him.
> Canker is a disease of plants,
> Cancer one of animals.
>
> (10)

After Stephen's fall into the polluted ditch, these sentences echo through his feverish head: "Canker was a disease of plants and cancer one of animals: or another different" (21). Other meanings associated with the word *canker* make the metaphor an especially appropriate one in Joyce's autobiographical novels. A canker is also a sore that spreads and will not heal. A cankerworm bores into fruits or flowers and destroys them. A canker is any corrupting element.

Joyce was later to expand the associations of this word to include any bug or insect. Just as in *Ulysses* Bloom's metaphorical bee sting suggests infection with venereal disease, so too in *Finnegans Wake* do stings and bites of insects indicate the moment of infection. Joyce employed the existing literary convention of the insect bite as a metaphor for sexual intercourse (for example, "The Flea" by John Donne) and carried it one step further to represent sexually transmitted disease. Similarly in *Finnegans Wake* Joyce used Gogarty's jibe about the canker, a hackneyed expression in turn-of-the-century literature, and with a twist of imagination and humor converted it into the earwig.

According to folklore, the earwig entered the ear of a sleeping person, penetrated the eardrum and destroyed the brains of its victim (Levin 155). Not unlike "a poison poured in the porch of a sleeping ear," the earwig was believed to cause its host to be "done to death in sleep," never knowing the "manner of his quell." Actually, the earwig, as the term is used in England, is a bug that enters the bud of flowers and destroys the bloom—a lotus-eater—a canker that destroys plants. HCE is "quite a big bug after the dahlias" (596.27). The earwig is a perfect metaphor for human disease. But Joyce does not stop there. By extension, all insects, especially biting ones, can symbolize the transmission of disease from one person to another. Fritz Senn has seen a correlation between the words insects/incest, but I would suggest that other possible associations are insects/in sex/infects ("Insects Appalling"). The brothers Shem and Shaun are "bread by the same fire, . . . tucked in the one bed and bit by the one flea" (168.8-10), and the lovers Tristan and Isolde are "exchanging fleas from host to host" (394.18-19). Paul Leon wrote to Sylvia Beach on 19 April 1932 mentioning "a Joyce's insectfable," a term coined by Joyce himself (Ltr. at SUNY Buffalo). The fable referred to may have been that of the Ondt and the Gracehoper, but the term can also apply to all of *Finnegans Wake*.

Throughout the *Wake*, we find mention of ears, of earwigs, of fleas, lice, bugs, beetles, chiggers, ticks, termites, weevils, lightning bugs, fireflies, firebugs and, of course, maggots, ants, and grasshoppers, and a "bittersweet crab, a little present from the past" (170.7-8). We also find references to the dung beetle, the scarab, which to the ancient Egyptians was a sacred symbol of resurrection and immortality.

One can imagine the fun Joyce must have had thinking up puns and jokes about bugs for this "Eyrawyggia saga . . . of poor Osti-Fosti" (48.19). His humor here, as in *Ulysses*, is dark, for this is the saga "of the persins sin" (48.16). The fall of Finn is a "tragoady" (5.13). "In the buginning," Joyce tells us, "is the void" (378.29). "Thundersday" is followed by "flyday" (5.24). After his fall, Finn is transformed into an Earwicker, who "suffered from a vile disease" (33.17), from an "infamous private ailment (vulgovarioveneral)" (98.18), from a "pecuniary ailment . . . because souffrant chronic from a plenitude of house torts" (241.7). As Joseph Campbell pointed out many years ago, HCE's obscure disease is "suspiciously venereal" (*Skeleton Key* 7). Since he went "Jerusalemfaring in Arssia Manor" (suggesting wandering in a brothel), Earwicker is called "the journeyall Buggaloffs" but now "the loamsome roam to Laffayette is ended" (26.3-4, 15-16). Like Dante's Ulysses, like Icarus, like the sailors of Christopher Columbus, Finn MacCool also has wandered too far in forbidden realms, and as a consequence, he will undergo a series of transformations: "Finnish Make Goal! First you were Nomad, next you were Namar, now you're Numah and it's soon you'll be Nomon" (374.21-23). As Earwicker, the "first old wugger of himself in the flesh," he is "whiggissimus incarnadined . . . hibernating Massa Ewacka" (79.2-5). He is the "Vakingfar sleeper, monofractured by Piaras Ua Rhuamhilighaudhlug [Persse O'Reilly], tympan founder" (310.10-11). But while he sleeps, "The movibles are scrawling in motions, marching, all of them ago, in pitpat and zingzang for every busy eerie whig's a bit of a tory tale to tell" (20.21-23). The "Ballad of Persse O'Reilly" [Fr. *perce-oreille*] tells the story in capsule. Earwicker is a viking invader of Ireland, "And *Gall's curse* on the day when Eblana bay/Saw his black and tan man-o'-war." For the "heathen Humpharey/Made bold a maid to woo/ . . . The general lost her maidenloo! . . . When some *bugger* let down the backtrap of the omnibus/ . . . he caught his death of fusili*ers*/ with his *rent in his rears./ Give him six years*" (emphasis mine). Unfortunately the story does not end there, for

> 'Tis *sore* pity for his innocent poor children
> But look out for his missus legitimate!

When that frew gets a grip of old Earwicker
Won't there be earwigs on the green?
(Emphasis added.) (46.13, 27-30; 47.9-17)

Earwigs breed earwigs, so that "in the age when hoops
ran high . . . *Mal*married*dad*" in love with his wife, was "in
rearing of a *nore*whig" (emphasis added) (20.31-21.1). Likewise we find the pun "Noirse-made-earsy" (314.27). Some
time later the "grand*fallar*" has "a *pock*ed wife in a pickle
that's a flyfire and three lice nittle clinkers, two twilling bugs
and one midgit pucelle." And, furthermore, "the deadsea
dugong updipdripping from his depths, has been *repreaching*
[reproaching] himself . . . . these *sik*tyten years ever since . .
. . our old offender was humile, commune and *ensectuous*"
(emphasis added) (29.27-28, 22-24). For "the ear of Fionn
Earwicker . . . was the trademark of a broadcaster" (108.21-
22). He is infectious. He has become the "Communicator"
(535.36).

My theory is that *Finnegans Wake*, at one level of meaning, is Joyce's own life story told over and over again,
"tellmastory repeating yourself" (397.7), but told in a kind
of coded language. We do not understand it by concentrat-
ing "solely on the literal sense . . . to the *sore* neglect of the
enveloping facts themselves circumstantiating it" (emphasis added) (109.12-14). But the more we know of Joyce's
life story, of the facts "circumstantiating" the fictions, the
better our chances of finding the metaphors, the patterns,
the web of word associations that he uses to tell the story of
this "persins sin." Many of the images are bug-related; others are suggested by literary or mythic allusions, particularly by the legend of Finn MacCool.[1] At best I can hope
here to unravel a few threads, and to suggest one way of
reading the *Wake* based on image patterns and puns.

Joyce's method of constructing *Finnegans Wake* is, I believe, essentially the same as for *Ulysses*, that is two-plane,
mythic and comic (scatological). As Kimberly Devlin has
shown, close textual reading of *Ulysses* is probably the best
introduction to the *Wake* (*Wandering and Return in* Finnegans

Wake). I have pointed out in the preceding chapter that many of the same images of disease that occur in the earlier work reverberate throughout the later one as well. More surprising is that the mythic structure of *Finnegans Wake*, based on a Celtic, pre-Christian hero, should point to the same themes of sin and suffering, guilt and retribution, that we have encountered before, for these themes are neither Celtic nor pre-Christian. As with the legend of the Wandering Jew in *Ulysses*, Joyce uses the legend of Finn MacCool to suit his own purposes, retaining many elements of the original myth, or embroidering when necessary to fit his own design. Thus he transforms Finn into: "Great sinner, good sonner, . . . in effect the motto of the MacCowell family," and we are told, "The Coyle-Finns paid full feines for their sinns" (607.4; 330.17). Joyce's Finn, not the legendary one, bears much resemblance to the Wandering Jew and also to Joyce himself. He is the "gran Phenician rover" (197.30). HCE in one of his incarnations is the Norwegian captain ("nowedding captain") (325.27), and also the Flying Dutchman ("flyend of a touchman") (327.23). Like Leopold Bloom, he is "the bugganeering wanderducken . . . with his bellows pockets fulled of potchtatos," (323.1, 17). He is "some wandering hamalags out of the adjacent cloverfields of Mosse's Gardens" (43.2), "that roundtheworlder wandelingswight . . . ancient ere decrepitude" (77.36-78.2), who "wandered out of his farmer's health and so lost his early parishlife" (589.21). Wandering has destroyed his family nest: "O wanderness be wondernest!" (318.17).[2]

The evidence, both biographical and literary, that Joyce himself suffered from syphilis is massive. He documented his own ailments minutely in letters to friends and family. The question of whether he actually infected his wife and children is another matter. Here the evidence is less conclusive because their symptoms have been less fully documented. Also, because a syphilitic person is infectious to sexual partners only for approximately four years after contracting the disease, and because there is no way to ascertain at what time Joyce became infected (only when he was treated), it is difficult to know exactly when he would have been infectious to Nora. However, the fact that she was treated with arsenic in 1908 indicates a great likelihood that she was infected by that time. During periods of relapse, spirochete activity is greater and infectiousness increases. We recall that Joyce had been ill with iritis and "rheumatic fever" in 1907. Based upon my own study of the progress of syphilis (with the assistance of several physicians and many medical textbooks), I believe it possible, given the short time lapse between his treatment with mercury and his elopement with Nora, followed soon thereafter by the conception of their children, that he did infect them. Louis Gillet attests to Joyce's extreme anxiety over his children's health (similar to the concern of Gabriel Conroy in "The Dead") which suggests that Joyce too believed it possible: "Their minor illnesses, their coughs, the slightest of fevers that children are subject to, maddened him. From an early date he had to recognize with terror the alarming signs of a nervous disturbance in his daughter. How could an innocent creature, a beauty so young and naive, carry unknowingly in its body the germs that would destroy it?" (Potts 192). (Schizophrenia, let us note, is *not* caused by germs.) Even if Joyce did not infect his family, however, even if Lucia's mental derangement really was schizophrenia, even if Giorgio's health problems were totally unrelated to his father's history, even if Nora's hysterectomy had no connection to venereal infection, the *fear* that he was responsible for their illnesses, and especially for Lucia's insanity, certainly did haunt Joyce to the end of his days, and this fear and guilt is expressed in much of his later writing. In a letter to Harriet Weaver dated 9 June 1936, he explained, "Some mysterious malady has been creeping on both my children (the doctors are inclined to trace it back to our residence in Switzerland during the war) and if they have not succeeded in doing anything for themselves it is to blame, not they. My daughter's case is far the worse" (*Ltrs.* III: 386).

Bloom only suspected and feared that he might have been responsible for Rudy's death. Joyce, by the time he wrote *Finnegans Wake*, appears convinced that he had "infect[ed] the whole stock company of the house of the leaking Barrel" (510.17). A letter written by Paul Leon to Harriet Weaver in 1936 indicates the extent to which Joyce blamed himself for his daughter's illness: "every time I meet him some new origin of her condition has been discovered the only thing which does not vary is the fact that he is the culprit" (*Ltrs.* III: 287). Although *Finnegans Wake* tells other stories, such as Joyce's belief that Gogarty and his friends in Ireland had betrayed his secret, and his fears that Nora had been unfaithful, essentially the story that he confesses over and over again is the story of infection.

Just as Joyce made his Ulysses a Jew, so did he make his Finn a Viking, a seaman who bears some resemblance to Sindbad, a "bugganeering [bug in ear] wanderducken" (323.1). Actually, according to legend, Finn was the leader of a band of roving warriors, the Fianna, who protected Ireland's shores against invaders. However, it suited Joyce's purposes better to make Finn himself the invader. As Harry Levin has pointed out, the name Earwicker is of Scandinavian origin, probably a corruption of the poetic form of Erik (Eirikr) (Levin 155). Finn is "Erievikkingr" (326.7), "Vikeroy" (100.5), and the "viceking" (18.13), also "Festy king" (85.23). HCE is called "inwader and uitlander" (581.3). In his various transformations he is Norwegian, Jute, Dane and "tipperruhry Swede," a pun that Joyce must have chortled over (82.3). He is an Ostman, the name given to the Norse settlers in Ireland, a word which affords Joyce the opportunity to pun on the word *bone* and also on *host*, which contains the stem *ost*. Thus we have jokes such as "Ivor the Boneless" (100.25). and "Osti-Fosti" (48.19), and "Ostia, lift it! Lift it, Ostia!" (371). *Finnegans Wake* is called

"the drema of *Sorestost* Areas, *Diseased*" (emphasis added)
(69.14). The word *Norse* made it possible for him to intro-
duce the name of his wife, Nora, in puns, and the word
German, the idea of germs. The Russian General is "the
rackushant Germanon" (338.2), also "the rising germinal"
(354.34) and the "Ructions gunorrhal" (192.2). Shem, "the
grand germogall allstar," has an "invaded personality"
(176.20; 247.8). In "The Children's Hour," Finn is identified as "patriss [father] all of them by the glos on their *ger-
mane* faces" (emphasis added) (230.32). For he was the
"pantymammy's Vulking Corsergoth" at "The invision [in-
vasion] of Indelond [Ireland]" (626.27). "If Dann's dane,
Ann's dirty" (139.23). By their "sinsinsinning since the night
of time" they have created a "new world through the ger-
mination of its gemination from Ond's outset till Odd's end"
(505.9-12).

Like the Vikings in Ireland, Joyce's Finn is a builder of
cities, the founder of a dynasty. He is Fintan, the first man
in Ireland, who survived the deluge to become the progeni-
tor of the race (Knott 34-36), and also "Finglas since the
Flood," the subject of a book being composed by the Four
Masters. ALP comments satirically, in a voice that sounds
like Nora's, "That'll be some kingly work in progress" (359.5;
625.13). He is also the biblical Shem, son of Noah, who
survived the flood to found the Hebrew race. Joyce plays
upon the irony of these analogies, for "our pantriarch" is
also the "father of fornicationists"; "paternoster" is
"pesternost," as well as "Singabob, the badfather," and "Dirty
Daddy Pantaloons" (74.11; 4.12; 31.7; 596.10; 94.33-35).
As Shem he has an "inkbattle house" (176.31), which is the
"house O'Shea or O'Shame . . . known as the Haunted
Inkbottle . . . infested with the raps" (182.30). As HCE (hod,
cement and edifices, 4.26) he is the Masterbuilder, an allusion to Ibsen's play about an architect who is responsible
for the deaths of his children in a fire, and who, because of
the promptings of a woman, climbs to the top of a tower he
has built and falls to his own death. In *Finnegans Wake* "our

misterbilder" is "openly damned and blasted by means of a hydromine, system" (77.3). The House that he builds is a "House of Blazes," for "Our Farfar" is the "Arthor [author] of our doyne [dying]" (63.23; 52.16) and we are "heirs of his tailsie" (96.35). His is *The House That Jack Built*, a house threatened by the archetypal symbols of destruction, flame and flood: "flamenfan, the ward of the wind that lightened the fire that lay in the wood that Jove bolt" (80.27); and

> [HCE] such as he is, from former times, nine *hosts* in himself, in his *hydrocomic establishment* and his ambling limfy peepingpartner, the slave of the ring that worries the hand that sways the lamp that shadows *the walk* that bends to his *bane* the busynext man that came on the cop with the fenian's bark that *pickled his widow* that primed the pope that *passed it round* on the volunteers' plate till it *croppied the ears of Purses Relle* that . . . bucked the jiggers to rhyme the rann that *flooded the routes of Eryan's isles* from Malin to Clear and Carn*sore Point* to Slynagollow and cleaned the pockets and ransomed the ribs of all the listeners, leud and lay, that bought the ballad that *Hosty* made. (Emphasis added.) (580.24-36)

In the scene in the Tavern, HCE is urged to recount his history, "How you fell from story to story like a sagasand to lie." Again the story is the destruction of the house: "Kick killykick for the house that juke built! Wait till they send you to sleep, scowpow! By jurors's cruces! [Jesus Christ] Then old Hunphydunphyville'll be blasted to bumboards by the youthful herald who would once you were" (375.4-7). With childish rhymes, Joyce tells the story of his family's ruin: "Ena milo melomon, frai is frau and swee is too, swee is two when swoo is free, *ana malawoe is we!* [Anna is sick.] A pair of *sycopanties* with amygdaleine eyes, one old obster lumpky pumpkin and three meddlars on their slies. And that was how *framm Sin* fromm Son, *acity arose,* finfin funfun" (emphasis mine) (94.14-19). Again, the father is the one responsible for the family's undoing. Joyce's overwhelming sense of guilt is the substance of *Finnegans Wake.* "He has founded a house, Uru, a house he has founded to which he has assigned its fate" (136.11). In his own mind, the house that Joyce built was doomed to destruction. "The house of Atreox is fallen indeedust" (55.3).

If I am correct in believing that *Finnegans Wake* is a coded work, then one way to decipher the code is to find the recurrent images that Joyce uses and see what meaning he attaches to them. As with the thread of allusions to houses examined above, the references do not occur together but rather are sprinkled throughout the work, often at great distance from each other. Joyce taxed his readers' memories to the utmost. My task here is to gather the scattered images and bring them together, not in context, not necessarily in their given order, but in a sequence which indicates that they do form a coherence of their own. The threads run vertically, not horizontally. I hope that the reader of my work will be able to return to the *Wake* with an increased awareness of Joyce's method and a better ability to explicate a given passage, no doubt discovering other examples too numerous to be included here.

Most of the symbols come from literary or mythic sources, many of them at least remotely connected with the legend of Finn MacCool. For example, as already noted, the images of fire and flood signify destruction, and so the story begins: "On Baalfire's night of this year after deluge . . . " (13.36).

In legend, fire is associated with the enemy of Finn, Goll. (A curious and perhaps important coincidence is that the part of the spinal column affected by *tabes dorsalis* is called the "posterior columns of Goll.") We have already noted the allusions in "The Ballad of Persse O'Reilly" to "Gall's curse," a pun on the words *Goll* and *God*. In *Finnegans Wake* fire suggests, among other things, the redness and burning of disease. The Oxman, we are told, "has been pestered by the firebugs and the Joynts have thrown up jerrybuilding to the Devanses and Little on the Green is

childsfather to the City (Year! Year! And laughtears!) . . .
on the eve of Killallwho" (15.6-11). The devastation is caused
because of "*boney*'s unlawfully obtaining a *pierced* para*flamme*
and *clap*trap *fire*guard" (emphasis added) (84.33). "Were
they bonfires? No other name would at all befit them un-
less that. Bonafieries!" (501.27). We can see in this passage
puns on the name of Bonaparte (with whom Joyce identified as a young boy) and on the words *bone* and *fire*. Likewise, with the pun on "Burnham and Bailey" (71.21), Joyce
conflates Finn MacCool with Phineas Finn (Phineas T.
Barnham), elsewhere making the expected puns on the
name of Trollope. Joyce conflates his Finn with all the other
Finns he could think of in literature or myth, just as his
Ulysses was conflated with all other wanderers, and as the
Wandering Jew appears also in the guise of the Flying
Dutchman or Rip Van Winkle. Thus Mark Twain's *Huckle-
berry Finn* also appears, along with the telling pun "Mark
Time's Finest Joke," a literary work which is HCE's "*mio
colpo*" (455.29).

Fire imagery in the *Wake* creates an apocalyptic "flamend
floody flatuous world" (23.10). On "wildfires night," which
is reminiscent of the sexual fantasies rampant in "Circe,"
the torments of "toastingforks pricking prongs up the
tunnybladders" suggest the pangs of pox and "ach bad clap"
(90.28). Kevin's note tells us that "Force Centres of the *Fire*
Serpentine" (emphasis added) are "heart, throat, navel,
spleen, sacral, fontanella, intertemporal eye," again cata-
loging affected body parts, an echo of Bloom's stump speech
in "Circe" which we examined earlier (303, left margin 1-
7). As a result of fire, no more high-kicking dances will occur, "for a burning would is come to dance inane. Glam-
ours hath moidered's lieb and herefore Coldours must leap
no more" (250.16). Wildfire serves as a metaphor for contagion, because Finn, in Promethean fashion, has "brought
as [us] plagues from Buddapest; put a matchhead on an
aspenstalk and set the living a fire" (131.11). One of the
suggested alternative titles for ALP's Mamafesta is *The Flash*

that *Flies from Vuggy's Eyes has Set Me Hair on Fire* (106.26).
The idea of the mother also being set afire is emphasized
by other references: "When they set fire then she's got to
glow"; "She has even brent her hair"; ALP has "auburnt
streams" and is called "Auburn chenlemagne" (suggesting
dog's mange, caused by a parasite, which causes hair loss)
(52.21; 578.28; 139.23; 280.27). ALP's red hair links her to
Nora, who told Joyce's sister Eva that Jim had fallen in love
with her auburn hair (Ellmann Collection, Tulsa). We recall that Nora had problems with her hair falling out, problems alluded to in *Finnegans Wake*: "First she let her hair fal
and down it flussed to her feet its teviots winding coils"
(206.29). And just as the mother is burnt, so will the child
Hetty Jane "rekindle the flame on Felix Day" (27.11-14).
Joyce associates disease with hearthfires by references to
"keeping the home fires burning" and "ous of their freiung
pfann into myne foyer" and "let's stay chez where the log
foyer's burning" (474.16; 538.26; 244.11). He also equates
it with hell's fire by puns on "Hellfeuersteyn" and
"monbreamstone" and "ethernal fire" and "overlusting fear
[ever lasting/lusting fire/fear]" (225.24, 22; 527.23;
222.30). Fire is also associated with the Phoenix, the fiery
bird that is resurrected from the ashes, that "disembers"
(24.11). The Phoenix is a perfect example of a Joycean symbol, on the mythic level signifying rebirth and eternal life;
on the historical, the Phoenix Park murders; on the scatological, a burning penis signaling the return of disease: "O
foenix culprit!" (23.16). Everyone has lots of "funn at
Flammagen's Ball. Till Irinwakes from Slumber Deep"
(321.17). Like Finn MacCool, the Phoenix sleeps, to awaken
in "red resurrection" (62.19).

Redness, rosiness, blush, or red spots are also images which
can signify disease. A red rash is one of the prominent symptoms of secondary syphilis. Jaun's Irish curse suggests such
a rash: "may the maledictions of Lousyfear fall like
nettlerash on the white friar's father that converted from

moonshine the fostermother . . . that ran off after the trumpadour" (439.6-9). The color red is associated with whores, for HCE has danced with "apple harlottes" (113.16). Then subsequently, "Mas marrit, Pas poulit, Ras *rudd*ist of all, though *flamifesto*uned [flame-infested] from galantifloures is *hued* and cried of each's *coulour*" (emphasis added) (256.8). Bloom's son, we recall, was named *Rudy*. When Finn's son is born, the narrator exclaims, "Eric aboy! And it's time that all paid tribute to this massive mortality, the *pink* of punk [punk being slang for prostitute] perfection as photography in mud" (emphasis added) (277.23). The name Finn means white or fair, an association Joyce makes clear by calling him "towhead," and "Whitehed," and "an old Whiteman self, the blighty blotchy," after he got "the miner smellpex" (40.25; 535.22; 263.8-9). When he is transformed, the whiteman undergoes a change of color. As Unfru-Chikda-Uru-Wukru he has "that blushmantle upon him from earsend to earsend" (24.9). As the Norwegian captain, he is "Burniface" (315.9), and as Dermot he is "Derg rudd face" with "Redspot his browbrand. Woman's the prey!" His mark resembles the mark of Cain, "The tarrant's brand on his hottoweyt [hot white] brow" (582.28-32; 583.29-30).

Dermot of the Love Spot is the young man whom Finn MacCool's betrothed, Grania, loved in preference to the aging Finn because he had a mark, a Love Spot, which made him irresistible to women. The story of Dermot, Grania, and Finn parallels that of Tristan, Isolde, and King Mark, and also that of Lancelot ("long alancey one"), Guenivere, and King Arthur (Our Father and "Arthor of our doyne") (360.34; 52.16). Joyce conflates the three love triangles, thus tripling the number of names on which he can pun and to which he can link other allusions. In these triangles, Dermot/Tristan/Lancelot seem to represent Joyce as a young man, whereas Finn/Mark/Arthur are the aging Joyce, just as Stephen and Bloom in *Ulysses* represent the author at different stages of his life. Dermot is "dearmate" and "diremood" and "Dammad" and also "redtom" (125.6, 8; 291.24; 21.31). His lover is "Groany" and "grannewwail" and "Graunya of the chilired cheeks" and "Grinny" who "sprids the boord [brood]" (291.24; 22.12; 7.9). The love spot of Dermot becomes "lovespots" in *Finnegans Wake*, and the prankquean washes "the blessings of the lovespots off the jiminy," the child, the diminutive of Jim (21.27).

The episode of the prankquean is, I believe, another of the parables in the *Wake* about the infection of the children. Here Joyce conflates the story of Grace O'Malley with the ancient Irish tale of the Fate of the Children of Lir, whose evil stepmother transforms them into swans, one of whom was named Fionnuala (Gregory 124-136). The metaphors tell the story. The prankquean (*quean* being harlot; see McHugh *Annotations* 21) "pulled a rosy one . . . And she lit up and fireland was ablaze" (21.15-17). As she kidnaps each of the three children, the same number that Joyce fathered, the last being a "blank" or a "dummy," she says, "Mark the Wans . . . . Mark the Twy . . . . Mark the Tris," and each child is transformed. Tristopher becomes a luderman, Hilary a tristian, and "the duppy shot the shutter clup [followed by sounds of the thunder, or the Fall]" (23.5). The names Tristopher and tristian are puns on Tristan, who is referred to as "Tristis Tristior Tristissimus" (Latin *trist* meaning sad), and who is called "sad hero" (158.1; 398.29).

The word *Mark* refers to the aging king to whom Isolde is unfaithful, but it has other references as well, such as to the disciple Mark, one of the four evangelists, who is referred to elsewhere in the *Wake* as "*Poor Mark!*" and whose portrait is to be found in *The Book of Kells* (see figure 3). It also refers to the novel *Jim the Penman*, published in 1901 by an Irish writer, Dick Donovan, pseudonym for Joyce Emerson Preston Muddock. The subtitle of the novel is *The Life Story of One of the Most Astounding Criminals that Ever Lived*. Along with the play also entitled *Jim the Penman* (1903) by Sir Charles L. Young, it provides the model for one of

Figure 3. The Apostle Mark from *The Book of Kells* (courtesy of the Board of Trinity College, Dublin)

the sons of HCE, Shem the Penman, the character Joycean critics have generally agreed to be a caricature of the author himself. In both works, by Donovan and by Young, Jim the Penman is a forger (in real life a man named James Townsend Savard; see McHugh *Annotations* 181) who gains great wealth by his talents. In the novel, however, the banks try to foil the criminal by using first an elaborate water*mark* on the banknotes, thinking that he will not be able to replicate this mark of identification, then by making perforations in the notes. In each case, the master criminal outwits the authorities and creates forged checks which no expert can distinguish from the originals. These two images, that of the mark and of the puncture, provide Joyce with two more metaphors for infection by sexual contact.

We know that Joyce was familiar with the play by Sir Charles Young because in 1924 he wrote Sylvia Beach asking her to obtain for him a copy of the old play *Jim the Penman* (*Ltrs. to Beach* 47). Only the internal evidence of *Finnegans Wake* indicates that he knew about Muddock's novel. However, in Trieste, according to Stanislaus, Joyce read another of Muddock's novels, so being familiar with the author, he probably knew the other work as well (Ellmann Collection, Tulsa). In the chapter on ALP's Mamafesta, among the distinguishing marks which identify the letter as the work of Shem the Penman are "paper wounds . . . perforations" and "waterungspillfull" (124.3, 23, 24).

These two images, of puncture and of stain (or mark or sign), recur throughout *Finnegans Wake* as part of an elaborate system of associated images which signify the sin of Finn MacCool. Over and over again, the sexual connotations of the piercing of the eardrum by Persse O'Reilly are repeated: "So lent she him ear to burrow his manhood (or so it appierce)" (512.23); "Yseen here the puncture. So he done it" (299.19); "And the prankquean went for her forty years' walk in Turnlemeem and she punched the curses of cromcruwell with the nail of a top into the jiminy . . . and she provorted him . . . and he became a tristian" (22.14-17); "That was the prick of the spindle to me that gave me the keys to dreamland" (615.27). As one might expect, Joyce makes many references to pricks.

His use of the image of the mark is more subtle and more complicated. The mourners at the wake tell Finn that he is "prime*signed*" in the full of his dress (24.28). The *stains* on Earwicker's shirt will not wash out no matter how hard the washerwomen scrub, and he and his carousing friends bear "several of the *earmarks* of design," earmarks which seem to be associated with "clap" (emphasis added) (66.1; 65.34). The ear of Fionn Earwicker, we recall, was the *trade-*

mark of a broadcaster (108.22). Similarly we find references to the "*dogmarks*" of origin, the "*penmarks*" on the sinscript that Shem has written and Shaun has carried, a letter which bears the "*watermark*" of a woman, and a "*teastain*" (emphasis added) (161.8; 421.18; 112.32; 111.20).

In the melodrama *Jim the Penman*, James Ralston, a master forger, has ruined his best friend by stealing his money, breaking up his romance, and marrying the girl himself. Each of the lovers receives a letter, forged of course, from the other calling off the engagement. Not until many years later, when the friend visits the married couple's home and the former lovers compare letters, do they learn they have been cheated out of their relationship. When the wife sees a cheque on which her husband has very skillfully signed her name, she realizes that he is the villain who forged the letters. He is also, it turns out, a criminal who has posed as a respectable businessman and who lives in fear of losing the admiration of the community and of his family. The villain's crimes are punished as if by divine retribution when he suffers a fatal heart attack just as his evil deeds are about to be revealed. In *Finnegans Wake*, Joyce conflates the discovery of the forged letters and cheque from this play with another discovery of evildoing, this time from the nineteenth-century gothic novel by an Irish writer, Sheridan LeFanu, *The House by the Churchyard*. Here the discovery is a skull unearthed in the graveyard which clearly indicates that murder has been committed. Joyce's combination of these two dissimilar literary works suggests first, that the husband is the villain and second, that the mysterious crime committed by (or perhaps perpetrated on) Earwicker in Phoenix Park is murder. Just as allusions to the Childs murder reverberate throughout *Ulysses*, the theme of murder echoes in *Finnegans Wake*. Phoenix Park, the historical site of a political assassination, was also located near Chapelizod, the site of the murder in LeFanu's novel.[3] The nature of HCE's crime is made clear in the following passage, in which Joyce also expresses his terror over Lucia's "fall": "That's all murtagh [murder] purtagh but what ababs [about] his dopter [daughter]? . . . The lappel of his size? [apple of his eyes] . . . he sicckumed of homnis terrars . . . . There were no peanats in her famalgia so no womble [womb/wonder] she tumbled" (314.30-36).

In the *Wake*, the discovery of the crime is made by means of a letter, which the hen unearths in a Dungheap, a letter which "has acquired accretions of terricious matter whilst loitering in the past. The *tea*time*stained* terminal . . . is a cosy little brown study all to oneself . . . whether it be *thumbprint, mademark* or just a *poor trait of the artless* [portrait of the artist], its importance [is] in establishing the identities in the writer complexus [identity of the complex writer]" (emphasis added) (114.28-33). When HCE remembers making love with his wife, he uses similar imagery: "I *thumbed* her with the iern of Erin and tradesman*marked* her lieflang mine for all and singular, iday, igone, imorgans and for ervigheds [forever]" (emphasis added) (547.33).

The thumbprint points to the identity of the writer as Finn MacCool, who in his youth, while cooking the sacred salmon of knowledge for the poet Finneces, burnt his thumb and put it into his mouth, thus gaining the power of divination (Cross and Slover 365). Joyce makes allusions to thumbs and salmon frequently in the *Wake*, punning on the word "salmen" (Fr. *sale* meaning dirty) and "salmofarious germs" which swim, we recall from his letter to Harriet Weaver, in the dirty waters of the Liffey (just as germs swim in the bloodstream) (264.17; 79.32). Anna Livia wears stockings that are "salmospotspeckled" and the bedroom of HCE and ALP has "Salmonpapered walls" (208.12; 559.2). HCE, Finn's first reincarnation, is the "samesake subsubstitute of a hooky salmon" (28.35) and "as for the salmon he was coming up in him all life long" (132.35). Shem's "salmonkelt's thinskin" indicates that he too bears a close relationship to Finn, only in lowlier form yet (169.19). Like Leopold Bloom's decline from Virag to Bloom to Flower, with each transformation, Finn is diminished. After his fall, the "Almost rubicund Salmosalar . . . smolten in our mist, woebecanned and packt away," becomes "goodridhirring" (7.16-19).

The mark on the letter that the hen finds is the most ingenious and the most convoluted complex of images that Joyce uses to tell his personal story. The letter is "this oldworld epistola of their weatherings and their marryings and their buryings and their natural selections [which] has combled tumbled down to us fersch and made-at-all-hours like an old cup on tay" (117.27). (It is important to note that the teastained letter is again associated with a cup of tea.) In one sense, the letter represents *Finnegans Wake*. "It is told in sounds in utter that, in signs so adds to, in universal, in polyglutteral, in auxiliary neutral idiom, sordomutics, florilingua, sheltafocal, flayflutter, a *con's cubane*, a *pro's tutute*, strassarab, *ereperse* and anythongue athall" (emphasis added) (117.12-16). The letter "was folded with cunning, sealed with crime, uptied by a harlot, undone by a child" (94.8). It is also "a letter to a king about a treasure from a cat," cat being, as in *Ulysses*, an uncomplimentary identification of woman, in this case as source of infection (278.16). Tea is associated with a biting insect: "Tick for Teac" (139.29). Tea is also "for a tryst" (119.30). Frequently the two images of letter and tea occur together: "the gossiple so delivered in his *epistol*ear, buried *tea*toastally in their Irish stew;" the letter contains a "pee ess from . . . affectionate largelooking *tache of tch* (Fr. "spot" of tea, suggesting urine). The stain, and that of a *teastain* (the overcautelousness of the masterbilker here, as usual, signing the page away), *marked* it off *on the spout* of the moment as a genuine relique of ancient Irish pleasant pottery;" and "*Madges Tighe*, the postulate auditressee, when her daremood's a grownian [Dermot and Grania], is always . . . hoping to Michael for the *latter* [letter] to turn up with a *cupital tea*" (emphasis added) (38.23; 111.18-23; 369.30-32). Both images, that of the letter and of tea, are related to Maggie (slang for pros-

titute; see McHugh *Annotations* 106): "a letter to last a lifetime for Maggi" and "Let a prostitute be whoso stands before a door and winks or parks herself in the fornix near a
makeussin wall (sinsin! sinsin!) . . . sweet tarts punch hell's
hate into his twin nicky and that Maggy's tea" (211.22;
116.15-23). Both Madges Tighe and Maggy's tea are puns
on the word *majesty*: "that variant maggers for the more
generally accepted majesty" (120.17), which suggests Finn
MacCool, the viceking, also maggoty mag and "His Magnus
Maggerstick" (535.7).

Brenda Maddox suggests, facetiously I am sure, that
there are enough references to tea in Joyce's work to fill a
doctoral dissertation, and she emphasizes the importance
of the ritual of teatime in the Joyces' family life, Nora being proud of her strongly brewed tea. Let us assume then a
correlation between Nora and teastain (and also between
Joyce and urine). It is the hen, the mate of the cock, who
finds the letter, which is a "loveletter," a "cloudletlitter," a
"redletter" (80.14; 73.29; 50.31). What then does this
"cupital tea," or capital T, represent? Adaline Glasheen
pointed out years ago that "throughout *Finnegans Wake*
[Joyce] follows Ibsen's early play *Love's Comedy* and equates
tea and sexual love" (173). Joyce gives us a clue that it is "a
word as cunningly hidden in its maze of confused drapery
as a fieldmouse in a nest of coloured ribbons" (120.5). We
have already found the word Salvarsan concealed in a pun.
Another such word is hidden, I believe, in the nonsensical
phrase "*Trip* over sacramental *tea*" (440.21). (Similarly, the
word *syphilis* is cleverly concealed in several passages:
"*Phyllis*citations to daff Mr. Hairwigger"; "whi*ss*le when
Phyllis floods her stable"; "cyphalos"; and "mick-
roo*cyphyllicks*" (emphasis added) (491.30; 60.4; 422.7; 525.8-
9).) In older medical textbooks, *Treponema pallidum*, the spirochete which causes syphilis, was written *T. pallidum*. It is a
T for a tryst, a T associated with sexual love, a T acquired
from a Maggie, a letter to last his majesty's lifetime. The
question, "was he in tea e'er he went on the bier . . . ?" is

followed by "He sent out Christy Columb and he came back with a jailbird's unbespokables in his beak" (496.28-31). Tea will account for the fall of Finn MacCool.

Very carefully, Joyce directs us to the Tunc page of *The Book of Kells* (or Book of Kills) where we find the graphic image of the letter T, "strange exotic serpentine . . . [which] seems to uncoil spirally and swell lacertinelazily before our eyes under pressure of the writer's hand" (121.20-25), a phallic image, but one with enormous teeth (see figure 4). (According to Quetel, a Spanish nobleman in the court of Ferdinand and Isabella described the new sickness that had appeared after the voyages of Columbus as the "serpentine sickness" [35-36].) We recall that it is Fire *Serpentine* which centers on "heart, throat, navel, spleen, . . . intertemporal eye." This is God's curse, for "the Muster of the Hoose . . . called down on the Grand Precurser who coiled him a crawler of the dupest dye and thundered at him to flatch down off that erection and be aslimed [ashamed] of himself for the bellance of hissch leif [balance of his life]" (506.5-8). The spirochete affords Joyce the opportunity for puns on spirals (Spira in Me Domino), curls (poison cerls and twinned little curls), worms (would you puff the earthworm outer my ear), and wagtails (wiggywagtail, and how are you, yaggy? With a capital Tea for Thirst) (485.19; 331.18; 491.31; 509.29; 302.9).[4] HCE is a "Human Conger Eel," an association with the letter T that is made more explicit by "congorool *teal*" (525.26; 165.21). "Mynfadher" is also a "boer constructor" (180.35). The "Initials majuscule of Earwicker" are "a round thousand whirligig glorioles" (119.14-17). The image of the "Big Whiggler" conflates the earwig with the serpent (284.25). Joyce also puns on a large number of words associated with the letter T: already noted are "scalding *tay*boil" and "heirs of his *tail*sie," but in addition are "nouveau*tays*," "Greenland's *tay*," "Kersse the *taler*," and "Houseanna! *Tea* is the Highest. For auld lang ayterni*tay*!" (emphasis added) (435.12; 199.18; 406.28). Furthermore, Joyce reveals who is responsible for spilling

Figure 4. Letter T from the Tunc page of *The Book of Kells* (courtesy of The Board of Trinity College, Dublin)

the tea: "that salubrated sickenagiaour of yaours have teaspilled all my hazeydency. Forge away, Sunny Sim!" (305.3-5), his own nickname as a boy being Sunny Jim. (The use of the pun on *hesitency* [*sic*] links this letter also to the forged letter that was used to try to incriminate Charles Parncll, Joyce's boyhood idol. The misspelling of the word was what identified the letter as a forgery.)

The letter found by the hen is not the only letter to appear in *Finnegans Wake*. The children sent a Nightletter to their parents, with their best "youlldied [yuletide/you all died] greedings," wishing them "very merry Incarnations"

(308.17). The children are, in a sense, the incarnations of
Joyce's daughter Lucia, with her "myriads of drifting minds
in one," the new letter, a pun on Nuvoletta, over whose fate
"there fell a tear, a *sin*gult [single/sin guilt] tear" (emphasis
added) (159.5-13). At the end of "The Children's Hour,"
Joyce encloses a prayer for his children (259.3-6) (emphasis added):

> O Loud, hear the wee beseech of thees of each of
> these thy unlitten ones! . . .
> That they take no chill. That they ming no merder.
> *That they shall not go*meet *mad*howiatrees.

The nineteenth-century Irish playwright Dion Boucicault
provided Joyce with two more important images for
Finnegans Wake from his play *Arrah-na-Poghue.* One is the
character Shaun the Post, the upright, sanctimonious foil
for his nasty brother Shem. Shem and Shaun serve, in one
sense, as do many other of the paired male characters in
the *Wake,* such as Mutt and Jute, and the Ondt and the
Gracehoper, Justius and Mercius, as two aspects of Joyce's
personality warring with each other, in Freudian terms, his
id with his superego, in Christian terms, his conscience with
his sexuality. Their battles consist largely of the superego
flagellating the id, and the id responding by defending itself verbally and nonviolently. The character of Shaun is
also modelled, as many critics have noted, on Joyce's critical brother Stanislaus, as can be seen in the following passage: "Enchainted, dear sweet Stainusless, young confes-
sor, dearer dearest . . . You are Pure. You are in your puerity.
You have not brought stinking members into the house of
Amanti" (237.25). *Amanti* suggests love, based on Fr. *amant*
(lover), but also *amenti,* the name given by the ancient Egyptians to the abode of the dead. Shaun, let us note, despite
his purity, is a letter carrier.

In Boucicault's play, Arrah (Irish for *Nora*) saves the
life of a young man who has been unjustly arrested by giv-

ing him a kiss (Ir. *poghue*) in which she passes a note from her mouth to his. This is the primary symbol which Joyce takes from the melodrama, making puns on "bouch-icaulture" (Fr. *bouche* meaning mouth) and "lacessive kiss" (lacerating/lascivious/cesspool), indicating the mouth as a culture of bacteria (569.35; 68.12). One agnomen of HCE's is "Hotchkiss Culthur's Everready" (523.14). The kiss is an appropriate metaphor for the transmission of syphilis, for during the secondary stage of the disease, moist lesions form in the mouth which can literally enable a person to transmit the spirochete by kissing. (In Gogarty's play *Blight*, Medical Dick and Medical Davy discuss this means of spreading infection.) HCE's kiss is a "poghue puxy" (83.33). He is "The bog which puckerood the posy" (604.3). Likewise, Issy, his daughter, says, "there's a key in my kiss" (279n.8). Like the insect bite, or the bitch bite at the ear, the kiss, especially one in which a substance is transferred (like Molly's seedcake), suggests sexual intercourse. After his fall Finn is "becrimed, becursekissed and bedumbtoit!" from his encounter with "ivargraine jadesses with a message in their mouths" (78.32; 19.23). The reference reinforces the idea of woman as the source of infection. However, in the chapter on the "big kuss of Trustan with Usolde" the male is the source of contagion. It is "*his* poghue like Arrah-na-poghue," *his* "mouth of mandibles" that is "poghuing her scandalous and very wrong . . . under the *sy*amores" until "The eitch is in her blood, arrah!" (emphasis mine) "Those were the grandest gynecollege histories" (383.18; 384.34; 385.2; 388.23; 376.19; 389.9). The lover's kiss is literally the kiss of death. After Tristan makes love with Isolde, "It was so scalding sorry for the whole twice two four of us" (389.32).

One reason that Joyce uses Tristan and Isolde as his archetypical lovers, rather than Dermot and Grania, who are more closely related in legend to Finn MacCool, is to emphasize the theme of love and death. Associated with the lovers is Wagner's *Liebestod*, which begins *Mild unde leise*.

Joyce puns on this phrase with "mildew Lisa" and "his mild dewed cheek" and "mild aunt Liza." He has ALP refer to HCE as "my life in death companion." The puns on mildew also suggest another form of parasite (40.17; 57.27; 388.4; 201.8).

Finnegans Wake is very much a *Book of the Dead*, a title on which Joyce puns early in the work, calling it "the boke of the deeds, annals of themselves timing the *cycles of events*" (13.30). *The Book of the Dead* describes the cult of Osiris, "Irise, Osirises" (493.28), the Egyptian resurrection god, whose sister/widow Isis appears in the *Wake* as "Madame Isa Veuve La Belle" (Fr. *veuve* meaning widow) (556.9). The name *Issy* conflates Iseult (young lover) with Isis (sister and wife). The death and immortality of Osiris are conflated with the resurrection of Tim Finnegan and of Finn MacCool, the legendary hero who sleeps until Ireland's moment of need, at which time he shall awaken. As indicated in the preceding chapter, Finn's sleep in the *Wake* represents, at one level of meaning, the dormant stages of his disease from which he awakens repeatedly, each time in worse condition than before. He has been changed from wine to vinegar; to alloy from allay; from Brian Boru at Clontarf to Bruyant le Bref at Dungtarf; from Finn to Earwicker to Shem; from Shaun to Jaun to Yawn. He is a "human pest cycling (pist!) and recycling (past!) about the sledgy streets, here he was (pust!) again!" (99.4). His final transformation will be death.

Not all of the transformations in *Finnegans Wake* point to disease, however. Barbara di Bernard has noted the many references Joyce makes to alchemical transformations. Stanislaus tells us that as a young man Joyce had studied Hermetic lore that was circulating in Dublin at that time, a lore that originated with the ancient Egyptians (*MBK* 140-41). We recall that Bloom was a Freemason. In the *Wake* Shem the Penman is an "alshemist" (185.35). The goal of the alchemist was to find the philosopher's stone, which would grant long life and freedom from disease to whoever attained it, and which would also transform base metals into gold. Titus Burckhardt, in his book on the alchemical tradition, maintains, however, that the metallic images were only symbols for the "transmutation or rebirth of the soul of the artist himself," that alchemy, though not a religion in itself, was "one particular means of access to the full meaning of the eternal and saving message of revelation" (23, 21). The references to alchemical transformations, like the allusions to *The Book of the Dead*, point to a theme of spiritual rebirth. The recurrent image of the Phoenix, as we have seen, represents resurrection of the flesh, signifying both the return of disease and eternal life, and in the seventeenth century, the Phoenix was a symbol of Christ, who also arose from the dead. Likewise, the lowly dung beetle (which Shem resembles, being "this dirty little blacking beetle") was to the ancient Egyptians the sacred scarab, symbol of resurrection and immortality because it was believed to roll its ball of dung through the netherworld and then to reappear alive (171). Joyce refers to it in *Finnegans Wake*: "Ladies did not disdain those pagan ironed times of the first city (called after the ugliest Danadune) when a frond was a friend inneed to carry, as earwigs do their dead, their soil to the earth-ball where indeeth [indeed/in death] we shall calm decline, our legacy unknown" (79.14). And the Ondt exclaims, in reference to the Gracehoper, "scarab my sahul!" (415.25). Thus the insect imagery, linking the Gracehoper with the scarab, reinforces the theme of hope for eternal life. Joyce himself was a "gracehoper," or, as he told Harriet Weaver, "one who hopes for grace" (*SL* 332). Again we see the scatological plane and the spiritual plane of Joyce's work intersect.

Another suggestion of spiritual transformation in *Finnegans Wake* was made some thirty years ago by Henry Morton Robinson in an article entitled "Hardest Crux Ever." Robinson pointed out the necessity of solving the meaning of the initials of HCE if we are ever to understand the larger work. He suggested that the Latin words of consecration in the Mass, "Hoc Est Enim Corpus Meum," and "Hic Est Enim

Calix Sanguinis Mei" provide an answer to the crux. To the faithful Catholic, these words signify that the bread and wine undergo transubstantiation, literally change in substance into the body and blood of Christ. The answer Robinson proposes would fit in with the general theme of transformation that appears throughout the *Wake*. We recall Bloom stretching out in the bathtub, pronouncing the words of consecration, "This is my body," over his flaccid flesh. The *double entente* points both ways, to physical and to spiritual transformation.

As Joyce completed this, his last work, with the pain from his disease increasing, his strength declining, he was anticipating his own last transformation, death, and thinking about a spiritual life beyond, "with his can of Tea . . . waiting for the end to come" (392.31-33), waiting "in wish and wish in vain till the grame reaper draws nigh, with the sickle of sickles, as a blessing in disguise" (457.9-10). At the end of *Finnegans Wake*, as the river of life flows out to sea, Anna Liffey's words express the feelings of the dying man as he anticipates meeting his Creator: "Loonely in me loneness. For all their faults. I am passing out. O bitter ending! I'll slip away before they're up. They'll never see. Nor know. Nor[a] miss me. And it's old and old it's sad and old it's sad and weary I go back to you, my cold father, my cold mad father, my cold mad feary father" (627.34-628.2).

In essence, *Finnegans Wake* is a religious work of literature. The refrain of the ballad from which it takes its title goes, "Wasn't it the truth I've told ye? Lots of fun at Finnegan's Wake." Joyce echoes the question, "isn't it the truath I'm tallin ye?" (15). As David Wright has noted, this last work is Joyce's most complete and direct confession (115). He has answered another question in the ballad, "Macool, Macool, orra whyi deed ye diie?" He has told all his sins, "for tough troth is stronger than fortuitous fiction" (279), and in making his confession, he has prepared to meet that cold mad feary father. Catholics are taught that if before death they make a perfect act of contrition, their sins will be forgiven, even mortal sins. Joyce repented. Words such as "I'm terribly sorry, I swear to you I am," (144.35) and "I'm sorry! I saw. I'm sorry!" (581.24) and "*mio colpo*" (455.27) and "meac Coolp, Arram . . . I confesses withould pride" are utterances buried throughout the work. Not only is *Finnegans Wake* Joyce's confession, but this final work is also his last act of contrition.

Epilogue: Dear mysterre Shame's Voice

In 1929 Shakespeare and Company published a collection of essays on *Finnegans Wake*, written by Joyce's friends and entitled *Our Exagmination round His Factification for Incamination of Work in Progress*. This anthology contains a letter which Richard Ellmann says is "obviously composed if not written by Joyce himself but never acknowledged by him" (*Ltrs.* III: 187n). It is a comic epistle, written in puns and portmanteau words and parodying the style of the *Wake*, supposedly from a bewildered reader to Joyce, asking him to explain the meaning of his difficult work. Delivered by post to Sylvia Beach's bookshop, the letter was signed Vladimir Dixon, the name of a writer who actually lived in Paris in the 1920s and who died in 1929, a writer whose initials, appropriately, are V.D.

In the Spring 1992 edition of *The James Joyce Quarterly*, which was devoted to solving the identity of the mysterious Vladimir Dixon, John Whittier-Ferguson proves Dixon's knowledge of the letter, but certainly does not "prove beyond the shadow of a doubt," as Robert Spoo suggests, that Dixon was the author of the letter (472). It would have been quite possible for Joyce to compose the letter and then implicate Dixon in his little joke. The internal evidence of the letter points to Joyce himself as its author. It is doubtful that anyone else, much less a person virtually unacquainted with Joyce, could have made numerous puns alluding to his illness and to his sick children. Yet the letter contains a pun on illness/illnest, which is very similar to the pun wanderness/wondernest that Joyce makes on page 318.17 of the *Wake*.

At Joyce's urging, Sylvia Beach included the Vladimir

Dixon letter at the end of *Our Exagmination*. It begins with a telling pun on Joyce's name: "Dear Mister Germ's Choice." My supposition is that within this anthology of scholarly essays, which were written supposedly to clarify for his readers the meaning of *Finnegans Wake*, Joyce cunningly planted a clue to his gigantic word puzzle. The puns, "I have been so strichnine [stricken/poisoned] by my illnest" and "some ass pecked which is Uncle Lear", repeat the images of poison, illness, the genital wound, and the affliction of the family that we have encountered in *Ulysses* and in *Finnegans Wake* (*Ltrs.* III: 187-88). These images provide clues to the nature of the illness that affected the children of Lir. Even more significant, however, are the puns on Joyce's name, the second being, "dear mysterre Shame's Voice". Just as "Germ's Choice" points to the physical malady from which he suffered, "Shame's Voice" indicates his spiritual and mental anguish. His is the voice crying out "in gutter dispear" (suggesting both "utter despair" and "gutter + loss of spear," another allusion to Joyce's condition of which Vladimir Dixon would presumably have been unaware).

For centuries venereal infection has been viewed by society as a cause for shame, as something more than a physical disease, as God's punishment for sexual sins. By the stigma attached to it, society punishes its victims emotionally just as harshly as nature does physically. When syphilis first broke out in Europe, syphilitics were turned away from regular hospitals and quarantined like lepers, for fear that they would spread their infection (Quetel 24-25). Like AIDS victims in our own times, they were shunned and castigated.

Joyce feared the opprobrium and, perhaps worse, the ridicule that accompanied public knowledge of the dreaded disease. This may explain why he left Ireland to become an exile on the European continent. He believed, probably rightly so, that Gogarty had told others about his affliction and that he, like Bloom and like HCE, was the butt of jokes circulating the pubs of Ireland, as evidenced by Gogarty's ribald ballads about the poxy sailor Sindbad, pumped full of mercury, and about the medical student who suffered

from gonorrhea. I suspect that even today a good number
of people in Ireland have heard about Joyce's illness. The
doctors who first raised questions about the nature of his
maladies are Irish.

Likewise, Irish writers frequently allude to Joyce and
to syphilis in the same penstroke. For instance, Flann
O'Brien's humorous *At Swim-Two-Birds* satirizes, among
other things, Joyce, secluded in Paris, writing *Ulysses* and
Finnegans Wake in bed. Such satire would be better understood in Ireland than in the rest of the world: "Was Trellis
mad? It is extremely hard to say. Was he a victim of hard-
to-explain *hallucinations?* Nobody knows. Even experts do
not agree on these vital points. Professor Unternehmer, the
eminent German *neurologist,* points to Claudius as a lunatic
but allows Trellis *an inverted sow neurosis* wherein *the farrow
eat their dam.* DuFernier, however, Professor of Mental Sci-
ences and Sanitation at the Sorbonne, deduces from a *want
of hygiene in the author's bed-habits* a *progressive weakening of the
head*"(emphasis added) (314-15). The implication, that the
author Trellis may be suffering from paresis, is the same
insinuation that Dr. Joseph Collins, a prominent American
neurologist with an Irish name, wrote about Joyce in his
review of *Ulysses* for *The New York Times* and in his book *The
Doctor Looks at Literature.* In O'Brien's later novel, *The Dalkey
Archive,* it is a Dr. Crewett who reveals the *strictly confidential*
information that James Joyce is still alive and living in Ireland. In the course of conversation, the doctor refers to the
discovery of penicillin, which, it is noted, has been effective
"in the treatment of a great many diseases" (101). The main
character, Mick, learning of Joyce's whereabouts from the
doctor, goes in search of him, only to find "a great writer
. . . gone queer in the head." He says about Joyce, "mim-
icry and mockery were usually among the skills of the intel-
lectually gifted; indeed, it was generally true that precision
in playing a role ordained by *morbid cerebral hypostasis is characteristic of most persons troubled in the mind*"(emphasis added)
(187-88).

Samuel Beckett's paired characters, Lucky and Pozzo,

Ham and Clov, each contain a personage bearing some distorted resemblance to the great artist in his infirmities, particularly Ham, the blind, invalid storyteller who urinates in his pants.

Another Irish writer who associates Joyce with syphilis is poet Patrick Kavanagh, who began publishing in the 1930s. He wrote one poem entitled "Joyce's *Ulysses*" which contains the lines:

> But thoughts are sin and words are soiled
> And Nietzschean blood is syphilitic.
> [*Collected Poems* 120]

Another of his poems, "Portrait of the Artist," which certainly suggests Joyce by its title, portrays a great artist who

> Wrote a play,
> Got the pox,
> Made a film,
> Wrote the incidental music.
> [121]

Given the usually unsympathetic attitude of the general public toward syphilis, is it any wonder that Joyce should have fled Ireland, where his malady was known, then used all his cunning to deceive the world as to the nature of his ailments? Or that his friends and relatives should have shielded him, and perhaps destroyed evidence for him, to prevent the truth from becoming generally known? Frank Budgen suppressed letters pertaining to Lucia (Tulsa, corresp. with Ellmann); Harriet Shaw Weaver, Nora, and Stephen Joyce all are known to have destroyed letters; in 1991 when the Paul Leon Papers in the National Library in Ireland came out from under seal, Stephen Joyce confiscated materials pertaining to his Aunt Lucia before anyone else was allowed to see them; and two boxes of the Jolas Papers at Yale are under seal until the year 2019.

It is ironic that Joyce's foremost biographer, Richard Ellmann, should have met with so much family resistance, not to his biography of Joyce, which does not mention that

Joyce contracted syphilis, but to his last work, on Oscar Wilde, in which he stated his belief that Wilde suffered from that disease. The attempt to tell the truth about so delicate a matter will naturally elicit a protective reaction from friends and heirs.

During an author's lifetime, or while the relatives whom he might have infected are still alive, such a protective attitude may be justifiable. But why should it continue now, when all the principles of the Joyce family drama, save Stephen, are dead? What is the fear? That the revelation that Joyce suffered from syphilis will somehow diminish his literary achievement? On the contrary, many writers have made their physical condition a part of their art, whether directly or indirectly. Witness Adrienne Rich writing about the pain of arthritis, or Yeats about the anguish of old age. And just as our recognition that Keats was a young man dying of tuberculosis and Synge of lymphosarcoma helps us to respond to their sense of the brevity of life and love, just as our knowledge of Milton's blindness enhances our sympathy for *Samson Agonistes,* so too does our understanding of Joyce's illness add a dimension of poignancy to his works which has hitherto been obscured by his humor. Furthermore, why should we consider one disease to be a legitimate concern of criticism more than another? The body, all of the body, as Joyce insisted, is a part of life which cannot be deemed to exist outside the domain of art.

Suffering is a furnace that expands the soul and tempers the steel of the pen. One might even argue that Joyce was a greater writer because of the ordeal he endured. Certainly without this experience he would have been a different artist. Compare the quality of his writing in *Stephen Hero,* the novel he began before he left Ireland in 1904, with the revised version, *A Portrait of the Artist as a Young Man,* written after his affliction with "rheumatic fever" in 1907. Consider how much more powerful is the later work, and how much greater the irony of that work, if we know the consequences of Stephen's sexual and spiritual liberation. The truth does not diminish the works but enhances them.

Willard Potts, in his introduction to *Portraits of the Artist in Exile,* raises the question of whether Joyce had syphilis and then asks, dismissing his own question, what difference does it make? I would answer that it can make an enormous difference in our understanding of the works. Since the publication of *Ulysses* in 1922, James Joyce has been one of the most enigmatic writers of the Western world. He misled his readers to view *Ulysses* as primarily Homeric and comic. Armed with the *Odyssey* in one hand and Ellmann's biography in the other, generations of scholars have tried to comprehend and interpret the cryptic writings of this duplicitous man. In the first case, Homer provides only a partial mythic analogue, and in the second, Ellmann furnishes an incomplete construct of the artist's life and personality, a portrait of "Sunny Jim" grown older. In both, the darker side is omitted, or at least minimized. Without knowledge of the mental suffering Joyce experienced because of his disease, readers have been unable to see the deeper implications of his works. The notes of pain and grief and pathos that permeate his writing have gone ignored or have been laughed away in a flood of scatological jokes. Joyce once said to Marxist critic Adolph Hoffmeister: "My work, from *Dubliners* on, goes in a straight line of development. It is almost indivisible, only the scale of expressiveness and writing technique rises somewhat steeply. . . . The difference . . . comes from development and from that alone. My whole work is always *in progress.*"

The line of development delineated in my own work here is biographical, an attempt to compensate for omissions in the life story. For more than five decades, critics have been trying to decipher *Finnegans Wake,* or as Clive Hart describes his own efforts, to see the *Wake* as a whole and to determine where its center lies ("*Finnegans Wake* in Adjusted Perspective"). The reason for this, I believe, is that without an adequate construct of Joyce's life, we have not had the context in which to see the whole work.

On one hand, Joyce tried hard to keep the nature of his illness from the public; on the other, he seems to have wished the truth someday to be known. Why else would he have strewn so many clues throughout his writings? True, his confessions were made for his own emotional relief, but he also wrote for an audience that he must have hoped would someday understand and forgive, that would someday treat him with the enlightened compassion that a man deserves who has paid so dearly for his youthful folly and who has left so poignant and powerful a record of his remorse. It is time that the world should consider the suffering, the grief, the guilt that lay behind the laughter of this poor man, "mysterre Shame's Voice," who told the truth in *Finnegans Wake.*

Chronology of Joyce's Medical History

1882, Feb.	James Joyce is born.
1896 or 1898	At age fourteen or sixteen, has first experience with prostitutes.
1902, Dec.	Writes his mother about illness and a "curious weariness."
1903, Feb.	Has attack of vomiting and "neuralgia."
1904, March 10	Gogarty writes congratulating Joyce on receiving the "stigmata" and writes Dr. Mick Walsh asking him to treat Joyce for "gleet."
May 3	Gogarty writes Joyce poems about pox and mercury.
June 16	Joyce has first date with Nora Barnacle.
July	Composes first story, "The Sisters," about a priest stricken with paralysis.
Sept.	Resides with Gogarty in Martello Tower.
Oct.	Elopes with Nora to the continent.
Dec. 28	Writes that Nora is pregnant, that he is having cramps in the stomach, and that "my sight is lamentable."
1905, Feb.	Is wearing glasses.
April	"My health is not very good."
July 27	Giorgio Joyce is born.
Oct. 15	Joyce suffers "severe gastrical disarrangement."
Oct.	Composes story "Grace"; Stanislaus joins Joyce and Nora in Trieste.
1906, Aug.	Joyce, Nora, and Giorgio depart for Rome.
Sept.	"I wish I was not so weak physically sometimes."
Oct. 4	After reading Gogarty's article on venereal disease in Ireland, Joyce finds phrase "venereal ill-luck" more appropriate than "venereal excess."
Nov. 6	Suffers indigestion and constipation: "four or five days since I had the pleasure of defecating."

Nov. 13	There are "few mortals in Europe who are not in danger of waking some morning and finding themselves syphilitic."
Late 1906	Begins drinking heavily in Rome; begins plans for *Ulysses*.
Dec. 7	"My glasses annoy me."
Dec. 24	"Nora is about to have another child."
1906-7	Composes "The Dead."
1907, Feb. 11	"All this trouble . . . always finds its way into the bosom of my stomach."
March	Family returns to Trieste; Joyce begins severe bouts of drinking and suffers iritis, neuralgia, and stomach problems, culminating in "rheumatic fever" in summer of 1907.
July 26	Lucia Joyce is born.
Sept.	Joyce begins rewriting *Stephen Hero* into *Portrait of the Artist as a Young Man*.
1908, April	Completes first three chapters of *Portrait*.
May	Suffers another bad attack of iritis.
July	Nora, again pregnant, is given "arsenical medication."
Aug. 4	Nora suffers miscarriage.
1909, Aug.	Joyce returns to Ireland, where acquaintances are shocked by his loss of weight.
Oct.	Suffers sciatica and iritis in Ireland; also visits prostitutes again and has recurrence of venereal disease.
1909 and thereafter	Experiences minor bouts of rheumatism and iritis.
1913, Dec.	Acquaintance with Ezra Pound encourages Joyce to resume work on *Portrait*.
1914	Completes *Portrait*, writes *Giacomo Joyce*, begins *Exiles* and *Ulysses*.
1915, July	Writes Pound that his eye problems are the consequence of malarial fever.
1916, Oct.	Suffers "nervous collapse" in Zurich.
1917, Feb.-June	Has more severe attacks of "rheumatic iritis"; develops glaucoma and synechia.
Aug.	Nora takes children to Locarno, where she suffers from "nerves" and hair loss; Joyce has severe eye

attack in Zurich, undergoes first eye surgery, an iridectomy.

1918 Joyce is ill nine weeks with eyes.

1919, April Is still suffering recurrent attacks of iritis.

Late 1920
-early 1921 Is "plagued by violent neuralgia."

1921, Aug. Eye attack is followed by collapse at a theatre.

Oct. Finishes writing *Ulysses*.

1922, May Has severe eye attack in Paris.

Aug. Eyes are worse in London; doctors want to operate.

1923, March Begins writing *Finnegans Wake*.

April Has infected teeth extracted: Dr. Borsch performs sphincterectomy on eye.

1924, April Suffers "nervous collapse" from overwork.

June Dr. Borsch performs second iridectomy on left eye to forestall glaucoma; Joyce says his health was undermined by poison.

Aug. Stannie writes about "softening of brain."

Nov. Sight is worse; Dr. Borsch operates for cataract.

1925, April Undergoes eye surgery, a capsulectomy on left eye.

Dec. Undergoes two eye surgeries by Dr. Borsch; sight is growing progressively worse.

1926, Nov. Pound writes Joyce about a "new cure for clapp."

1926-28 Joyce suffers "nervous collapses" but no new eye attacks.

1928, April "I have lost pounds and pounds of flesh."

Sept. Is ill again with eyes.

Oct. Has a "large boil" on his arm; doctors give three-week course of arsenic and phosphorus injections, find "everything normal except his nerves."

Nov. Nora is operated on; receives seven days of radium treatment.

1929, Jan. Joyce's sight grows worse rapidly; Borsch wants to perform two more operations.

Feb. Nora has hysterectomy; "Dear Mister Germ's Choice" letter composed.

May Lucia ends dancing career because she lacks physical stamina to continue.

1930, March Joyce suffers a series of "fainting fits" lasting only a few seconds; lightness in head.

May	Dr. Alfred Vogt at Zurich operates on left eye for "tertiary cataract"; sight improves slightly; optic nerve and periphery of retina are found normal.
Dec.	Giorgio marries Helen Kastor Fleischman.
1931, July	Joyce and Nora are legally married in London; Lucia begins to behave strangely.
1932, Feb.	Lucia throws a chair at Nora.
March	Lucia goes into a "catatonic" state in the Leons' apartment.
April	Joyce arranges for Lucia to see Dr. Fontaine and a nerve specialist.
May	Lucia has a "nervous breakdown"; is placed (temporarily) in a sanatorium a month later.
July	Joyce sees Dr. Vogt, who finds his right eye much worse (lens much calcified) and declares optic nerve and retina are no longer normal; Carl Jung sees Lucia.
Late 1932	Lucia's illness enters "messianic" phase.
1933, Jan.	Joyce suffers hallucinations of ear and eye.
July	Lucia goes into hysterics at train station.
Sept.	Joyce suffers intense stomach pains, is administered laudanum; pains persist intermittently for the rest of his life.
1934, Feb.	Lucia strikes Nora, is again interned in a sanatorium.
June	Lucia is administered fever treatment.
Sept.	Dr. Naeggeli, a blood specialist, sees Lucia in Zurich; an American doctor sees her at Kusnacht, observes shuffling gait.
1935, Feb.	Eileen takes Lucia to London to visit Harriet Weaver; Lucia runs away, sleeps in the streets.
March	Eileen takes Lucia with her to Bray; Lucia sets fire to the house, runs away, has to be institutionalized in England.
April	Giorgio is suffering from rheumatism.
June	Joyce writes Giorgio that Lucia is "infinitely better"; Lucia's handwriting shows signs of great nervous agitation.
1936, Feb.	Maria Jolas brings Lucia back to Paris; she is taken from home to a clinic in a straitjacket, is declared dangerous.

May	Giorgio has surgery on his thyroid gland.
1937, April	Joyce sees Dr. Vogt, who finds his sight much improved.
July	"Some doctors and people who saw Lucia lately agree that she is much better than two and a half years ago."
1938, Jan.	"Lucia unfortunately continues to have a disconcerting and persistent relapse."
Feb.	Joyce has "retinal congestion" in his left eye.
1939, April	"Lucia is still very ill."
Dec.	After arranging for Lucia's care, the Joyces depart from Paris to join M. Jolas at Saint-Gerand-le-Puy.
1940, Dec.	The Joyces depart for Zurich.
1941, Jan. 9	Joyce is seized with intense stomach pains in the night, is administered morphine, taken to the hospital the next morning.
Jan. 11	When X-rays show an ulcer of the duodenum, doctors operate, find perforated ulcers and peritonitis.
Jan. 12	Joyce weakens and goes into a coma.
Jan. 13	In early morning, Joyce dies in the hospital, alone.

Notes

Prologue

1. See Herring, "Richard Ellmann's *James Joyce,*" in *The Biographer's Art: New Essays,* ed. Jeffrey Meyers (London: Macmillan, 1989); Nadel, "The Incomplete Joyce" in *Joyce Studies Annual,* 1991; Kelly, "Stanislaus Joyce, Ellsworth Mason, and Richard Ellman: The Making of *James Joyce*" in *Joyce Studies Annual,* 1992; Levitt, "The Biography of Leopold Bloom" in *James Joyce Literary Supplement,* Spring 1993.

2. Ellmann personally tracked, obtained and preserved many of the materials dealing with the early years of Joyce's life, and he assisted Stanislaus's widow in cataloguing the cache of Joyce manuscripts and letters left in her possession upon the death of her husband, papers which were eventually sold to Cornell University, many of which Ellmann later edited and published. Although Ellmann has been faulted for relying too heavily on Stanislaus, he defended himself against this charge in a letter to Maria Jolas: "It is unfortunate that he is the only witness to a great many things. Don't think me too gullible—I am quite prepared to refute him if I can catch him out" (17 Aug. 1954, Beinecke).

3. When Maria had decided to turn the trunk over to Giorgio, Ellmann also pleaded with her to have the letters photocopied in the event that Giorgio or his son Stephen might want to destroy some of them or to sell them piecemeal. I have found no information as to whether or not they were ever copied. The trunk eventually became the possession of Stephen Joyce, who has admitted destroying some of his Aunt Lucia's letters.

4. Je ne pense pas que les renseignements très précis sur la maladie oculaire, dont était atteint M. James Joyce, puissent vous être utiles. D'ailleurs, en principe, le secret professionnel interdirait de vous les révéler.

5. Drs. Ronald E. Smith and Robert A. Nozik write: "The clinical course of many of these forms of ocular syphilis is one of

gradual worsening and progression from an initial iridocyclitis to the whole spectrum of luetic eye disease [which includes glaucoma]" (179); and "Progressive worsening of any form of uveitis should alert the clinician to the possibility of tuberculosis or syphilis" (*Uveitis: A Clinical Approach to Diagnosis and Management* [1983] 181). Likewise, the findings of Drs. Stewart Duke-Elder and Edward S. Perkins contradict those of Dr. Lyons:

> Late (tertiary) syphilitic uveitis, occurring in the tertiary stage of the infection is somewhat rarer than the early secondary type, but nevertheless in Moore's (1931) series of cases it was about equally common . . . . It may occur in the first or second year of the infection, and its appearance may be delayed for 20 or more years . . . but its onset averages 10 years after the primary chancre . . . . The inflammation may be mild or very severe, typically involving the entire uveal tract and, in contrast to the early type, relapses are common even when adequate treatment is administered. The prognosis is considerably more serious than in the former variety, for permanently damaging sequelae are not unusual and, especially when several relapses have occurred, a resultant complicated cataract, phthisis and blindness are not unknown. [*Diseases of the Uveal Tract* (1966) 298]

A third medical textbook, *The Eye and Its Diseases* (1936), edited by Dr. Conrad Berens, states: "In the 109 tertiary cases [studied] the iritis was the only clinical manifestation; in 54 of these patients there were 13 cases of neurosyphilis, 16 vascular affections, and 27 patients with diseases of the bones, joints, or skin. In the 29 cases with relapse the iritis was often the *only* manifestation, frequently in association with a *negative Wassermann reaction.* The association of relapse cases with neurorecurrences is not rare" (second emphasis added) (648).

    6. See Olney, *Metaphors of Self: The Meaning of Autobiography,* 8-9; Axthelm, *The Modern Confessional Novel,* 8-9.

Chapter 1 The Creative Daemon

    1. Joyce's attitude toward sin during his later years is well illustrated by a vignette in the *Autobiography* of William Carlos Williams: "As we started to drink another round, Bob McAlmon, who may have been a little tight, proposed, 'Here's to sin!' Joyce looked up suddenly. 'I won't drink to that,' he said."

2. Joyce also used this term in an earlier version (1904) of *Portrait of the Artist as a Young Man,* which ends with the words: "amid the *general paralysis of an insane society,* the confederate will issue in action" (emphasis added) (Ellmann Collection, Tulsa).

3. Gogarty refused, in 1954, to allow Ellmann to interview him for the Joyce biography (Ltr. at Tulsa).

4. Numbers given for this correspondence refer to Robert Scholes's catalogue of the Cornell Joyce Collection.

5. Et tout d'abord il [Joyce] écrit de manière à ce que personne ne le comprend, ni ne peut le comprendre . . . . Il s'était parfaitement amusant de traduire en formules incompréhensible des idées toutes simples et de croire que c'est peutêtre un chef d'oeuvre[*sic*].

Chapter 2 The Wandering Jew in *Ulysses*

1. For detailed studies of the legend, see Joseph Gaer's *The Legend of the Wandering Jew* or George Anderson's work by the same title.

2. Bloom smiles occasionally, but laughter exists only in his past. Stephen, on the other hand, laughs loudly. In Ellmann's miscellaneous notes is one of unspecified source: "No one could laugh so wholeheartedly as Joyce, or so infectiously." J.H. Byrne, one of Joyce's boyhood friends, commented on Joyce's laughter in 1933, when "James Joyce gave one of his, at that time, rare howls of laughter, and tears of merriment came into his poor eyes" (235).

3. Article by Waisbren and Hall is discussed earlier in Prologue. Whereas they catalogue many references to the syphilis in *Ulysses,* they do not attempt to explain the significance of these allusions to the meaning of the novel.

4. Whether or not Bloom is impotent has been a subject of critical debate. Marilyn French (*The Book as World* 148) and Suzette Henke (*Joyce's Moraculous Sindbook* 93n) both believe that he is, but French attributes this condition to guilt over Rudy's defectiveness, and Henke, because of Bloom's ability to masturbate, considers him to be suffering from "secondary impotence" due to anxiety or trauma. Morris Beja emphatically denies that Bloom is impotent because he "can clearly achieve erection and ejaculate, as he does by masturbating over Gerty MacDowell; and . . . he has performed coitus interruptus with Molly" ("The Joyce of Sex" 256). When I

use the term *impotence*, I refer to the ability not only to achieve an erection, but also to maintain it during intercourse. Bloom's problem, I believe, is his inability "To keep it up,/To keep it up" (5.283).

5. According to Quetel, the Japanese name for syphilis was "plum-tree poison" or "plum-tree ulcer" (52).

6. In *Narrative Con/Texts in* Ulysses, Bernard Benstock argues that there is no concrete proof that Bridie Kelly is a prostitute and suggests that the term "daughter of the night" may mean that Bridie Kelly is a Gentile and thus "an abomination." Benstock contrasts the earlier passage in "Oxen of the Sun" with the later fantasy in "Circe," in which Bridie, clearly in the role of prostitute in her second appearance, accosts Bloom on the streets. Benstock notes that the words that she uses in "Circe" are the same with which the prostitute solicits Stephen in *Portrait*: "Any good in your mind?" The prostitute who addresses Stephen, Fresh Nellie, was the name of a whore in one of Oliver Gogarty's ballads, "Fresh Nellie the Coalquay Whore," whose palate is perforated by a gumma of syphilis and whose nose was rotted off. Personally, I find no ambiguity in the reference to "daughter of the night" in "Oxen of the Sun." However, Benstock's observation on the similarity of the words of invitation in the two passages not only identifies Bridie in "Circe" as a prostitute, but also suggests that she is a poxy one.

7. If Bloom is suffering from *tabes dorsalis*, this would explain his partial impotence. According to Alex Comfort in *Sexual Consequences of Disability* (20), lesions of the lumbo-sacral cord can interfere "with reflexogenic erections but not necessarily with psychogenic erections. Consequently, complete impotence is a relatively uncommon symptom of *tabes dorsalis*."

8. According to Cecil (7th ed., 383), three out of four women with untreated syphilis of less than two years' duration will give birth to a syphilitic stillborn or living infant. According to Kampmeier (*Essentials* 413), 20 percent of the babies of untreated syphilitic mothers are born alive and free of syphilis; of the 56 percent born alive with syphilis, 25 percent die in infancy and 75 percent survive but may develop later manifestations.

9. According to Stanislaus Joyce's Trieste diary (20 and 23 June 1908), Nora accused Jim of being responsible for their children's eye infections because he "used to go with filthy women." She had been told so by her women friends.

10. I have been able to learn of no correlation between rheumatic fever and uveitis, nor between malarial fever and uveitis, yet every attack of rheumatic pains suffered by Joyce that Stanislaus describes is accompanied by uveitis. If these attacks were caused by increased spirochete activity, that would explain why the two problems repeatedly occurred simultaneously. Furthermore, as we shall see later, malarial fever was sometimes administered as treatment for neurosyphilis. If Joyce was ever given fever treatment, this might account for his slip of the pen to Ezra Pound.

Chapter 3 Epics of the Body

1. This is how Joyce saw himself. His correspondence with Marthe Fleischmann indicates that he too felt old before his time: "Moi, je suis vieux—et je me sens plus vieux encore. Peut-être ai-je trop vécu. J'ai 35 ans" (U. of Texas, Stuart Gilbert Collection). My translation: "I am old—and I feel older still. Perhaps I have lived too much. I am 35 years old." Likewise, to William Bradley he wrote: "[troubles] . . . have aged me prematurely. I now have a long flowing white beard with eye on fire [?], plumtree jam [?], and most weak hams" (4 March 1921, Cornell 6.058).

2. The person named Bradley to whom he refers here was William A. Bradley, an American literary agent who lived in Paris in the 1920s and with whom Joyce was acquainted. (See Stuart Gilbert's Paris journal, *Reflections on James Joyce* 4.) On September 10, 1920, just weeks before his correspondence with Budgen regarding the etymology of the word *syphilis,* Joyce wrote to Bradley inviting him to dine with him: "I should like very much to talk with you about the Circe episode which I am writing for the sixth time" (Cornell 6.049).

3. Maupassant, who was afflicted with the disease and eventually died of paresis, used a similar image. See Quetel 128.

4. Joyce may also have had in mind the superstition prevalent both in Ireland and in Trieste that a cure for syphilis could be effected by having sexual intercourse with a virgin. See Trieste Diary in Tulsa, entry of 2 October 1907.

5. Remember Gogarty's poem about Sindbad, the sailor in his Tertiaries.

6. The main character in "A Little Cloud" is named Chandler, which in Anglo-Irish means "maggot." See Wall 30.

7. Bernard Benstock has noted that the dreamer in *Finnegans Wake* "associated its [the letter's] message with the scurrilous ballad, the spreading gossip, the newspaper account and the radio skit. His guilty mind transforms its material into damaging evidence against him" ("Every Telling Has Its Taling" 18).

8. As a boy, Joyce greatly admired Napoleon, so that for him Waterloo signified the fall of a hero with whom he identified. Furthermore, historians have speculated that Napoleon himself was afflicted with syphilis. (See Will and Ariel Durant, *The Age of Napoleon* 238.) In her memoir, his daughter Lucia remembered that the family had visited Waterloo by car when they were in Brussels (U. of Texas). Joyce associated Oliver Gogarty with the Duke of Wellington because he was born on the street in Dublin where Wellington's family had lived (*It Isn't This Time of Year at All* 21). Thus, the "big wide h*arse*" of the "ironed dux" is a reference to Joyce's companion in whoring (emphasis added)(8.21). In *Finnegans Wake*, the adversarial relationship between Joyce and Gogarty is indicated, among other references, through allusions to the military rivals, Napoleon and Wellington. Joyce, it seems, blamed Gogarty for his Waterloo.

9. To my knowledge this letter is the earliest primary evidence that Joyce suffered with eye problems or wore glasses. Although Ellmann claims that Joyce was nearsighted as a small boy, and that he actually did have his glasses broken at school, the only source that he names is Joyce's account to Herbert Gorman (*JJ* 26, 28). Photographs of Joyce before 1904 include no eyeglasses.

10. In his personal correspondence, Flaubert also used the image of "the hero's scar" in reference to his own syphilitic infection. See Quetel 127-28.

11. "pyrifère, contre lequelle elle s'oppose violemment, mais elle parait être plus claire dans ses idées pendant sa fièvre."

12. In a letter to Richard Ellmann, dated 1 April 1959, Harriet Shaw Weaver wrote of Lucia's improved condition: "The doctors told me this improvement is due to tranquilising drugs they have been giving her, rather than to any radical improvement in her illness. Even so, it seems to me an excellent thing that she should be so much happier and more alert."

Chapter 4   An Insectfable

1. For a good study of the legend of Finn MacCool, and of Joyce's use of the legend, see James MacKillop's *Fionn mac Cumhaill: Celtic Myth in English Literature* (1986).

2. This pun is very similar to the one made in the letter to "Mister Germ's Choice," which we will examine later.

3. It is not clear whether in the episode in Phoenix Park, the site of the murder, Earwicker is the victim or the criminal. In one version of the episode, he meets a cad with a pipe, who is a "bissexcyclist," suggesting Oliver Gogarty, who won races in cycling. Stanislaus tells how Gogarty and his friends used to take the drunken, unconscious Jim out of taverns and deposit him in parks or other outdoor places to sleep off his stupor. Possibly Joyce blamed his ill health on Gogarty, believing that exposure to the elements had lowered his resistance to disease. In the *Wake*, Joyce writes: "Don't him forget! A butcheler [butcher/bachelor] artsed out of Cullege Trainity. Diddled he daddle a drop of the cradler on delight mebold laddy was stetched?" (315.1). Gogarty's degree was from Trinity College.

4. Long before the discovery of microbiology which made possible the identification of the infectious spirochete, doctors speculated whether syphilis could be caused by tiny worms (Quetel 79). Perhaps Joyce had researched the subject sufficiently to be acquainted with those archaic theories. Claude Quetel tells of one seventeenth century poet who compared the sickness to a "deadly worm which eats away the pith of a once sturdy tree which soon must fall to the axe" (74).

Bibliography

I. Unprinted Sources

My research for this study has been conducted at a number of repositories in the United States where some of Joyce's letters and manuscripts, or where papers of his friends and contemporaries, are located. At the University of Delaware I read Ulick O'Connor's collection for his biography of Oliver St. John Gogarty. At Wayne State University I saw photocopies of Joyce family correspondence, some of which is not to be found in this country. At the New York Public Library I spent time in the John Quinn Memorial Collection and in the papers of Adrienne Monnier. I have worked in the James Joyce Collection at SUNY Buffalo's Poetry/Rare Books Collection; in the Joyce Collection at Cornell's Olin Library; at Yale's Beinecke Library in the James Joyce Archive, and in the Ezra Pound Papers; in the Oliver St. John Gogarty Collection at Bucknell's Ellen Clarke Bertrand Library; and at the Library of Congress. Most recently, I have spent several weeks in the Richard Ellmann Collection at the University of Tulsa's McFarlin Library, in the Eugene and Maria Jolas papers in the Beinecke Library at Yale, and in the Joyce Collection and Stuart Gilbert Collection at the Harry Ransom Humanities Research Center at the University of Texas at Austin.

II. Printed Works

A. Literary

Anderson, George K. *The Legend of the Wandering Jew.* Providence: Brown UP, 1965.

Antheil, George. *Bad Boy of Music.* Garden City, New York: Doubleday, 1945.

Atherton, James. *The Books at the Wake: A Study of Literary Allusions in James Joyce's* Finnegans Wake. Carbondale: Southern Illinois UP, 1959.

Beach, Sylvia. *Shakespeare and Company.* New York: Harcourt, 1959.

Beja, Morris. *James Joyce, A Literary Life*. Ohio State UP, 1992.

——. "The Joyce of Sex: Sexual Relationships in *Ulysses*," in *The Seventh of Joyce*. 255-67. Ed. Bernard Benstock. Bloomington: Indiana UP, 1982.

Benstock, Bernard. "An Afternoon with Stephen Joyce." *James Joyce Literary Supplement* (Spring 1987): 7.

——. *James Joyce*. N.Y.: Frederick Ungar Publishing Co., 1985.

——. *Joyce-again's Wake: An Analysis of* Finnegans Wake. Westport, CT: Greenwood Press, 1965.

——. "Leopold Bloom as Dreamer in *Finnegans Wake*." *Critical Essays on James Joyce's* Finnegans Wake. Ed. Patrick A. McCarthy. N.Y.: G.K. Hall and Co., 1992.

——. *Narrative Con/Texts in* Ulysses. Urbana: U of Illinois P, 1991.

Benstock, Shari. "Is He a Jew or a Gentile or a Holy Roman?" *James Joyce Quarterly* 16 (1979): 493-97.

——. "Sexuality and Survival in *Finnegans Wake*." *Critical Essays on James Joyce's* Finnegans Wake. ed. Patrick A. McCarthy. N.Y.: G.K. Hall and Co., 1992.

Bernard, Barbara di. *Alchemy and* Finnegans Wake. Albany: State U of New York P, 1980.

Bishop, John. *Joyce's Book of the Dark*. Madison: U of Wisconsin P, 1986.

Blackmur, R.P. "The Jew in Search of a Son." *Virginia Quarterly Review* 24 (1948): 96-116.

Bluefarb, Sam. "Leopold Bloom's Jewishness." *Modern British Literature* 2 (1977): 18-84.

Book of Kells. Study of Manuscript by Francois Henry. New York: Knopf, 1974.

Boucicault, Dion. *Arrah-na-Pogue; or the Wicklow Wedding*. Chicago: The Dramatic Publishing Co., n.d.

Bowen, Zack. Ulysses *As a Comic Novel*. Syracuse UP, 1989.

——, and Paul Butera. "The New Bloomusalem: Transformations in Epiphany Land." *Modern British Literature* 3 (1978): 48-55.

Brandabur, Edward. "The Sisters." *Dubliners*. Viking Critical Edition. Ed. Robert Scholes and A. Walton Litz. New York: Viking, 1969.

Brandt, Allan M. *No Magic Bullet: A Social History of Venereal Disease in the United States since 1880*. New York: Oxford UP, 1985.

Brown, Richard. *James Joyce and Sexuality*. Cambridge UP, 1985.

Budge, E.A. Wallis. *The Book of the Dead: The Papyrus of Ani*. 1895. New York: Dover Publications, 1987.

Budgen, Frank. "Further Recollections of James Joyce," *Partisan Review*, pp 530-44.

——. *James Joyce and the Making of* Ulysses. Bloomington: Indiana UP, 1960.

——. *Myselves When Young*. London: Oxford UP, 1970.

Burchhardt, Titus. *Alchemy: Science of the Cosmos, Science of the Soul.* Baltimore: Penguin, 1960.

Byrne, John Francis. *Silent Years: An Autobiography with Memoirs of James Joyce and Our Ireland.* New York: Farrar, 1953.

Campbell, Joseph. "Contransmagnificandjew-bangtantiality." *Studies in the Literary Imagination* 3. 2 (Oct. 1970): 3-18.

——. *The Masks of God: Creative Mythology*. New York: Penguin, 1968.

——, and Henry Morton Robinson. *A Skeleton Key to* Finnegans Wake. 1944. New York: Penguin, 1980.

Carens, James F. "Joyce and Gogarty." *New Light on Joyce from the Dublin Symposium.* Bloomington: Indiana UP, 1972. 28-45.

——. *Surpassing Wit: Oliver St. John Gogarty, his Poetry and his Prose.* New York: Columbia UP, 1979.

Chadwick, Nora. *The Celts.* 1970. Middlesex: Penguin, 1979.

Cixous, Helene. *The Exile of James Joyce.* Trans. Sally A.J. Purcell. New York: David Lewis, 1972.

Collins, Dr. Joseph. *The Doctor Looks at Literature: Psychological Studies of Life and Letters.* 1923 by George Doran. Rpt. Port Washington, N.Y.: Kennikat Press, 1972.

——. Interview. *Columbia University Oral History Collection,* Microfiche 18.

——. "James Joyce's Amazing Chronicle." Review of *Ulysses. New York Times Book Review and Magazine.* 28 May 1922, 6+.

Colum, Mary and Padraic. *Our Friend James Joyce.* New York: Doubleday, 1958.

Colum, Padraic. *The Joyce we Knew.* Ed. Ulick O'Connor. Cork: Mercier Press, 1967.

Connolly, Thomas E. *The Personal Library of James Joyce: A Descriptive Bibliography.* U of Buffalo P, 1955.

Cross, Tom Peete and Clark Harris Slover. *Ancient Irish Tales.* New York: Holt, 1936.

Curran, Constantine P. *James Joyce Remembered.* New York: Oxford UP, 1968.

Dante Alighieri. *The Divine Comedy.* Trans. L. Bickersteth. Oxford: Basil Blackwell, 1972.

Davies, Stan Gebler. *James Joyce: A Portrait of the Artist.* New York: Stein and Day, 1975.

Davis, Roderick. "The Fourfold Moses in *Ulysses.*" *James Joyce Quarterly* 7 (1969-70): 120-31.

Devlin, Kimberly J. *Wandering and Return in* Finnegans Wake: *An Integrative Approach to Joyce's Fictions.* Princeton UP, 1991.

Donovan, Dick [Joyce Emmerson Preston *Muddock*]. *Jim the Penman: The Life Story of One of the Most Astounding Criminals That Have Ever Lived.* London: George Newnes, Ltd., 1901.

Eckley, Grace. *Children's Lore in* Finnegans Wake. Syracuse UP, 1985.

Eliade, Mircea. *The Myth of the Eternal Return or Cosmos and History.* Trans. Willard R. Trask. Bollingen Series. Princeton UP, 1954.

Eliot, Thomas Stearns. Preface. *My Brother's Keeper.* Stanislaus Joyce. New York: Viking, 1958.

———. "*Ulysses,* Order, and Myth." *Selected Prose of T.S. Eliot.* New York: Harcourt, 1975.

Ellenbogen, Eileen. "Leopold Bloom—Jew." *Changing World* 3 (1947-48): 79-86.

Ellmann, Richard. *The Consciousness of Joyce.* New York: Oxford UP, 1977.

———. *James Joyce.* New York: Oxford UP, 1982.

———. "Joyce and Homer." *Critical Inquiry* 3 (1977): 567-82.

———. *Ulysses on the Liffey.* New York: Oxford UP, 1972.

Epstein, E.L. "James Joyce and the Body," in *A Starchamber Quiry: A James Joyce Centennial Volume, 1882-1982.* 73-106. Ed. E.L. Epstein. N.Y.: Methuen, 1982.

Fisch, Harold. *The Dual Image: The Figure of the Jew in English and American Literature.* New York: Ktav Publishing House, 1971.

Fogel, Daniel Mark. "James Joyce, the Jews and *Ulysses.*" *James Joyce Quarterly* 16 (1979): 498-501.

French, Marilyn. *The Book As World: James Joyce's* Ulysses. Cambridge: Harvard UP. 1976.

Gaer, Joseph. *The Legend of the Wandering Jew.* New York: NAL, 1961.

Galli, Lina. "Reminiscence." *James Joyce Quarterly* 9 (1972) 334.

Gifford, Don. *Joyce Annotated: Notes for* Dubliners *and* Portrait of the Artist as a Young Man. 2nd ed. Berkeley: U of California P, 1982.

———. Ulysses *Annotated: Notes for James Joyce's* Ulysses. 2nd ed. Berkeley: U of California P, 1988.

Gilbert, Stuart. *James Joyce's* Ulysses. 1930. New York: Vintage Books, 1955.

Gillespie, Michael Patrick. *Reading the Book of Himself: Narrative Strategies in the Works of James Joyce.* Columbus: Ohio State UP, 1989.

Glasheen, Adaline. *"Finnegans Wake* and the Girls from Boston, Mass." *Hudson Review* Sp. 1954. Rpt. *Critical Essays on James Joyce's* Finnegans Wake. Ed. Patrick A. McCarthy. N.Y.: G.K. Hall and Co., 1992.

——. *Third Census of* Finnegans Wake: *An Index of the Characters and Their Roles.* Berkeley: U of California P, 1977.

Gogarty, Oliver St. John. *It Isn't This Time of Year at All: An Unpremeditated Autobiography.* Westport, Conn.: Greenwood Press, 1954.

——. "James Joyce: A Portrait of the Artist" in *Mourning Becomes Mrs. Spendlove and Other Portraits, Grave and Gay.* New York: Creative Age, 1948.

——. "James Joyce as a Tenor." in *Intimations.* New York: Abelard, 1950.

——. "The Joyce I Knew." *Saturday Review of Literature* 23. 14 (25 Jan. 1941) 3+.

——. *The Plays of Oliver St. John Gogarty.* Proscenium Press, n.d.

——. "They Think They Know Joyce." *Saturday Review of Literature* 33. 11 (18 March 1950) 8+.

——. *Tumbling in the Hay.* New York: Reynal & Hitchcock, 1939.

——. *A Week End in the Middle of the Week and Other Essays on the Bias.* New York: Doubleday, 1958.

Goldberg, Samuel. *The Classical Temper; A Study of James Joyce's* Ulysses. New York: Barnes and Noble, 1961.

Goldwasser, Thomas A. "Who was Vladimir Dixon? Was He Valdimir Dixon?" *James Joyce Quarterly* 16 (Sp. 1979) 219-22.

Gordon, John. *James Joyce's Metamorphoses.* Dublin: Gill and Macmillan, 1981.

Gorman, Herbert S. *James Joyce.* New York: Farrar, 1939.

Gregory, Isabella Augusta Persse, Lady. *Gods and Fighting Men: The Story of the Tuatha de Danaan and of the Fianna of Ireland.* New York: Oxford UP, 1970.

Gross, Harvey. "From Barabas to Bloom: Notes on the Figure of the Jew." *Western Humanities Review* 11 (1957): 149-56.

Hall, Vernon, Ph.D., and Burton A Waisbren, M.D. "Syphilis as a Major Theme of James Joyce's *Ulysses." Archives of Internal Medicine* 140. 7 (July 1980) 963-65.

Hart, Clive. *A Concordance to* Finnegans Wake. Mamaroneck, New York: Paul P. Appel, 1974.

———. *"Finnegans Wake* in Adjusted Perspective," in *Critical Essays on James Joyce's* Finnegans Wake. (15-33) Ed. Patrick A. McCarthy. N.Y.: G.K. Hall and Co., 1992.

———. *Structure and Motif in* Finnegans Wake. Northwestern UP, 1962.

Heilbrun, Carolyn. *Toward a Recognition of Androgyny.* Harper Colophon, 1973.

Henke, Suzette A. *James Joyce and the Politics of Desire.* London: Routledge, 1990.

———. *Joyce's Moraculous Sindbook: A Study of* Ulysses. Columbus: Ohio State UP, 1978.

Holloway, Julia Bolton. "Semus Sumus: Joyce and Pilgrimage." *Thought* 56 (1981): 212-25.

Hyman, Louis. *The Jews of Ireland from Earliest Times to the Year 1910.* Shannon: Irish UP, 1979.

James, Caryn. "Joyce Family Letters in Literary Debate." *New York Times* (15 Aug. 1988) Y13+.

Johnson, Paul. *Ireland: A Concise History from the Twelfth Century to the Present Day.* Chicago: Academy Chicago, 1980.

Joyce, James. *The Critical Writings.* Ed. Ellsworth Mason and Richard Ellmann. New York: Viking, 1966.

———. *Dubliners.* 1916. The Viking Critical Library. Ed. Robert Scholes and A. Walton Litz. New York: Viking, 1969.

———. *Finnegans Wake.* 1939. New York: Viking, 1976.

———. *Giacomo Joyce.* New York: Viking Press, 1968.

———. "The Holy Office." *The Portable James Joyce.* Ed. Harry Levin. New York: Penguin, 1976. 657-60.

———. *James Joyce's Letters to Sylvia Beach, 1921-1940.* Ed. Melissa Banta and Oscar A. Sullivan. Bloomington: Indiana UP, 1987.

———. *Letters of James Joyce, Volume I.* Ed. Stuart Gilbert. New York: Viking, 1957.

———. *Letters of James Joyce, Vols. II and III.* Ed. Richard Ellmann. New York: Viking, 1966.

———. *A Portrait of the Artist as a Young Man.* 1916. The Viking Critical Library. Ed. Chester G. Anderson. New York: Viking, 1981.

———. *James Joyce's Scribbledehobble: The Ur-Workbook for* Finnegans Wake. Ed. Thomas E. Connolly. Northwestern UP, 1961.

———. *Selected Letters of James Joyce.* Ed. Richard Ellmann. New York: Viking, 1975.

——. *Stephen Hero.* New York: New Directions, 1944.

——. *Ulysses.* The Corrected Text. Ed. Hans Walter Gabler. Vintage Books. New York: Random House, 1986.

Joyce, Stanislaus. *The Complete Dubllin Diary of Stanislaus Joyce.* Ed. George Harris Healey. Ithaca: Cornell UP, 1971.

——. *My Brother's Keeper: James Joyce's Early Years.* New York: Viking, 1958.

Kavanagh, Patrick. *Collected Poems.* New York: The Norton Library, 1973.

Kaye, Julian B. "A Portrait of the Artist as Blephen-Stoom." *A James Joyce Miscellany, Second Series.* Ed. Marvin Magalaner. Carbondale: Southern Illinois UP, 1959.

Kenner, Hugh. *Dublin's Joyce.* Bloomington: Indiana UP, 1956.

——. *Joyce's Voices.* Berkeley: U of California P, 1978.

——. *Ulysses.* London: George Allen and Unwin, 1980.

Knott, Eleanor and Gerard Murphy. *Early Irish Literature.* New York: Barnes & Noble, 1966.

Lawrence, Karen. *The Odyssey of Style in* Ulysses. Princeton UP, 1981.

LeFanu, Sheridan. *The House by the Churchyard.* 1863. New York: Stein and Day, 1968.

Leitch, Vincent B. "Myth in *Ulysses:* The Whirlwind and Hosea-Bloom." *James Joyce Quarterly* 10 (1972-73): 267-69.

Leventhal, A.J. "The Jew Errant." *Dublin Magazine* 2 (Sp. 1963): 11-24.

Levin, Harry. *James Joyce: A Critical Introduction.* Norfolk, Conn.: New Directions, 1941.

Levitt, Morton P. "A Hero for Our Time: Leopold Bloom and the Myth of Ulysses." *James Joyce Quarterly* 10 (1972): 132-34.

Lewis, Wyndham. *The Letters of Wyndham Lewis.* Ed. W.K. Rose. Norfolk, Conn.: New Directions, 1963.

Litz, A. Walton. *The Art of James Joyce: Method and Design in* Ulysses *and* Finnegans Wake. London: Oxford UP, 1961.

Lyons, J.B., M.D. *Oliver St. John Gogarty: The Man of Many Talents.* Dublin: Blackwater, 1980.

MacKillop, James. *Fionn mac Cumhaill: Celtic Myth in English Literature.* Syracuse UP, 1986.

McAlmon, Robert, and Kay Boyle. *Being Geniuses Together: 1920-30.* New York: Doubleday, 1968.

McCarthy, Patrick A. *The Riddles of* Finnegans Wake. Cranbury, N.J.: Assoc. University Presses, Inc., 1980.

————. Ulysses: *Portals of Discovery.* Twayne Masterwork Studies. Boston: Twayne Publishers, 1990.

McHugh, Roland, *Annotations to* Finnegans Wake. Baltimore: Johns Hopkins UP, 1980.

————. *The* Finnegans Wake *Experience.* Berkeley: U of California P, 1981.

————. *The Sigla of* Finnegans Wake. Austin: U of Texas P, 1976.

Maddox, Brenda. *Nora: The Real Life of Molly Bloom.* Boston: Houghton Mifflin, 1988.

Magalaner, Marvin. "The Anti-Semitic Limerick Incidents and Joyce's 'Bloomsday.'" *PMLA* 68. 2 (1953)" 1219-23.

Mahaffey, Vicki. *Reauthorizing Joyce.* Cambridge UP, 1988.

Mangan, James Clarence. "The Nameless One." *A Book of Ireland.* Ed. Frank O'Connor. London: Collins, 1959.

Manglaviti, Leo M.J. "Joyce and St. John." *James Joyce Quarterly* 9 (1971-72): 152-55.

Markson, David. "James Joyce's Jew." *Union College Symposium* 3 (Fall 1964): 10-12.

Morse, J. Mitchell. "Augustine, Ayenbite, and *Ulysses.*" *PMLA* 70 (Dec 1955): 1143-59.

Nadel, Ira B. *Joyce and the Jews: Culture and Texts.* London: Macmillan, 1989.

Noon, William T., S.J. *Joyce and Aquinas.* New Haven: Yale UP, 1957.

Norris, Margot. *The Decentered Universe of* Finnegans Wake. Baltimore: The Johns Hopkins UP, 1974.

O'Brien, Darcy. *The Conscience of Joyce.* Princeton: Princeton UP, 1968.

O'Brien, Flann [Brian O'Nolan]. *At Swim-Two-Birds.* 1939. New York: New American Library, 1976.

————. *The Dalkey Archive.* Normal, IL: Dalkey Archive Press, 1993.

O'Connor, Ulick. *The Times I've Seen: Oliver St. John Gogarty.* New York: Ivan Obolensky, Inc., 1963.

Post-structuralist Joyce: Essays from the French. Ed. Derek Attridge and Daniel Ferrer. Cambridge: Cambridge UP, 1984.

Potts, Willard, ed. *Portraits of the Artist in Exile: Recollections of James Joyce by Europeans.* Seattle: U of Washington P, 1979.

Pound, Ezra. *The Cantos.* New York: New Directions, 1956.

————. *Literary Essays of Ezra Pound.* New York: New Directions, 1968.

————. *Pound/Joyce: Letters of Ezra Pound to James Joyce with Pound's*

Essays on Joyce. Ed. Forrest Read. New York: New Directions, 1967.

Power, Arthur. *Conversations with James Joyce.* Ed. Clive Hart. New York: Barnes and Noble, 1974.

———. *The Joyce We Knew.* Ed. Ulick O'Connor. Cork: Mercier Press, 1967.

Prescott, Joseph. "The Characterization of Leopold Bloom." *Literature and Psychology* 9. 1 (1959): 3-5.

———. "Homer's *Odyssey* and Joyce's *Ulysses.*" *Modern Language Quarterly* 3. 3 (Sept. 1942): 427-44.

Raleigh, John Henry. "Bloom as a Modern Epic Hero." *Critical Inquiry* 3 (1977): 583-98.

Robinson, Henry Morton. "Hardest Crux Ever." *A James Joyce Miscellany, 2nd Series.* Ed. Marvin Magalaner. Carbondale: Southern Illinois UP, 1959. 195-207.

Ryan, J., ed. *A Bash in the Tunnel: James Joyce by the Irish.* London: Clifton Books, 1970.

Savio, Antonio F. "Reminiscence." *James Joyce Quarterly* 9 (1972) 32.

Schlossman, Beryl. *Joyce's Catholic Comedy of Language.* Madison: U of Wisconsin P, 1985.

Scholes, Robert. *The Cornell Joyce Collection: A Catalogue.* Ithaca: Cornell UP, 1961.

———, and Richard M. Kain, ed. *The Workshop of Dedalus: James Joyce and the Raw Materials for* A Portrait of the Artist as a Young Man. Evanston: Northwestern UP, 1965.

Schork, R.J. " "Nodebinding Ayes": Milton, Blindness and Egypt in the *Wake.*" *James Joyce Quarterly,* Fall 1992: 69-83.

Schutte, William. *Joyce and Shakespeare: A Study in the Meaning of Ulysses.* New Haven: Yale UP, 1957.

Scott, Bonnie Kime. *Joyce and Feminism.* Bloomington: Indiana UP, 1984.

Senn, Fritz. "Insects Appalling." *Twelve and a Tilly: Essays on the Occasion of the 25th Anniversary of* Finnegans Wake. 36-39. Ed. Jack P. Dalton and Clive Hart. London: Faber & Faber, 1966.

———. *Joyce's Dislocutions: Essays on Readings as Translation.* Ed. John Paul Riquelme. Baltimore: Johns Hopkins UP, 1984.

Shapiro, Leo. "The 'Zion' Motif in Joyce's *Ulysses.*" 1946. *Jewish Frontier Anthology, 1945-1967.* New York: Shulsinger Bros., 1967.

Shechner, Mark. *Joyce in Nighttown: A Psychoanalytic Inquiry into Ulysses.* Berkeley: U of California P, 1974.

Sheehy, Eugene. *The Joyce We Knew.* Ed. Ulick O'Connor. Cork: Mercier Press, 1967.

Spilka, Mark. "Leopold Bloom as Jewish Pickwick: A Neo-Dickensian Perspective." *Novel* 13 (Fall 1979): 121-46.

Stanford, W.B. "Ulyssean Qualities in Joyce's Leopold Bloom." *Comparative Literature* 5 (1953): 125-36.

———. *The Ulysses Theme: A Study in the Adaptability of a Traditional Hero.* 2nd ed. Oxford: Basil Blackwell, 1963.

Steinberg, Erwin R. "James Joyce and the Critics Notwithstanding, Leopold Bloom is Not Jewish." *Journal of Modern Literature* 9 (1981-82): 27-49.

Stephens, James. *James, Seumas and Jacques: Unpublished Writings of James Stephens.* Ed. Lloyd Frankenberg. New York: Macmillan, 1964.

St. Patrick: His Writings and Muirchu's Life. Ed. and transl. A.B.E. Hood. London: Phillimore and Co., 1978.

Thornton, Weldon. *Allusions in* Ulysses: *An Annotated List.* Chapel Hill: U of North Carolina P, 1968.

———. "Voices and Values in *Ulysses.*" in *Joyce's* Ulysses: *The Larger Perspective.* Ed. Robert D. Newman and Weldon Thornton. Newark: U of Delaware P, 1987. 244-70.

Tindall, William York. "Mosaic Bloom." *Mosaic* 6 (1972-73): 1-9.

Von Abele, Rudolph. "*Ulysses:* The Myth of Myth." *PMLA* 39. 3 (June 1954): 358-64.

Waisbren, Burton A., M.D. and Florence L. Walzl, Ph.D. "Paresis and the Priest: James Joyce's Symbolic Use of Syphilis in 'The Sisters.'" *Archives of Internal Medicine* 80. 5 (May 1974): 758-62.

Wall, Richard. *An Anglo-Irish Dialect Glossary for Joyce's Works.* Syracuse UP, 1986.

Whittier-Ferguson, John. "The Voice Behind the Echo: Vladimir Dixon's Letters to James Joyce and Sylvia Beach." *James Joyce Quarterly* (Spring 1992): 511-31.

Wilder, Thornton. "Joyce and the Modern Novel." *A James Joyce Miscellany* (1st). 11-19. Ed. Marvin Magalaner. N.Y.: Pub. Committee of the James Joyce Society, 1957.

Williams, William Carlos. *The Autobiography of William Carlos Williams.* MacGibbon and Kee, Ltd., 1968.

Woolf, Virginia. "Modern Fiction." *The Common Reader, First Series.* 1925. New York: Harcourt Brace Jovanovich, 1984.

Wright, David G. *Characters of Joyce.* Totown, N.J.: Gill and Macmillan, Barnes and Noble, 1983.

Yeats, William Butler. *The Autobiography*. New York: Collier Books, 1965.

——. *The Letters of William Butler Yeats*. Ed. Allan Wade. New York: Farrar, Strauss, and Giroux, 1980.

Young, Sir Charles L., Bart. *Jim the Penman: A Romance of Modern Society*. London: Samuel French, Ltd., 1912.

B. Medical

Adams, Raymond D., M.D. and Maurice Victor, M.D. *Principles of Neurology*. New York: McGraw-Hill, 1977.

Beck, Irving, A., M.D. "The Medical Odyssey of James Joyce." *Rhode Island Medical Journal* 69.11 (Nov. 1986): 517-22.

Berens, Conrad, M.D. ed. *The Eye and Its Diseases*. By 82 International Authorities. Philadelphia and London: W. B. Saunders Co., 1936.

Brandt, Allan M. *No Magic Bullet: A Social History of Venereal Disease in the United States since 1880*. New York: Oxford UP, 1985.

Campbell, Robert Jean, M.D. *Psychiatric Dictionary*. Oxford UP, 1989.

Cecil, Russell L., M.D. ed. *A Textbook of Medicine*. 7th ed. Philadelphia and London: W.B. Saunders Co., 1948.

Cecil Textbook of Medicine. Ed. James B. Wyngaarden, M.D. and Lloyd H. Smith, Jr., M.D. 16th ed. Philadelphia: W. B. Saunders Co., 1982.

Cleugh, James. *Secret Enemy: The Story of a Disease*. New York: Thomas Yoseloff, Inc., 1956.

Comfort, Alex. M.B., Ph.D., D.Sc. *Sexual Consequences of Disability*. Philadelphia: George F. Stickley Co., 1978.

Duke-Elder, Sir Stewart, G.C.V.O., F.R.S., and Edward S. Perkins, M.D. *Diseases of the Uveal Tract*. Vol. IX in *Systems of Ophthalmology*. London: Henry Kimpton, 1966.

Diagnostic and Statistical Manual of Mental Disorders. Third Edition, Revised. "DSM-III-R". American Psychiatric Association, 1987.

Elliott, Frank A., M.D. *Clinical Neurology*, 2nd ed. Philadelphia: W.B. Saunders, 1971.

Fabricant, Noah D., M.D. "The Ocular History of James Joyce." in *13 Famous Patients*. Philadelphia: Chilton Co., 1960.

Ford, William J., M.D. "James Joyce, An Artist in Adversity." *Quarterly Bulletin, Northwestern University Medical School* 23 (1949): 495-97.

Goodman, Louis, M.D. and Alfred Gilman, Ph.D. *The Pharmaco-*

logical Basis of Therapeutics. New York: Macmillan, 1941.

Kampmeier, Rudolph H., M.D. et al. *Essentials of Syphilology.* Philadelphia: J.B. Lippincott, 1943.

——. "Late and Congenital Syphilis." *Dermatologic Clinics* 1. 1 (Jan. 1983): 23-42.

Lyons, J.B., M.D. *James Joyce and Medicine.* Dublin: Dolmen, 1973.

——. "James Joyce's Miltonic Affliction, Pt. 1." *Irish Journal of Medical Science* 1. 4 (1968): 157-65.

——. "James Joyce's Miltonic Affliction, Pt. 2" *Irish Journal of Medical Science* 1. 5 (1968): 203-10.

——. *Thrust Syphilis Down to Hell and other Rejoyceana.* Dublin: Glendale Press, 1988.

——. *What Did I Die Of?* Dublin: The Lilliput Press, 1991.

Moore, Joseph Earle, M.D. et al. *The Modern Treatment of Syphilis,* 2nd ed. Springfield, Illinois: Charles C. Thomas Books, 1941.

Parran, Thomas, M.D. and Surgeon General of the U.S. Public Health Service. *Shadow on the Land: Syphilis.* New York: Reynal & Hitchcock, 1937.

Pusey, William Allen, M.D. *The History and Epidemiology of Syphilis.* Springfield, Illinois: Charles C. Thomas Books, 1933.

Quetel, Claude. *History of Syphilis.* Paris, 1986. Transl. by Judith Braddock and Brian Pike. Baltimore: The Johns Hopkins UP. 1990.

Sasse, Carl. "Dichter kampfen um ihr Augenlicht (James Joyce - Axel Munthe - Adolph von Hatzfeld)." *Cesra* (Dec. 1962): 224-28.

Shen, Winston W., M.D. and John J. Soldo, Ph.D. "Symbol Hunting in James Joyce's 'Syphilizations.'" Letter to editor. *Archives of Internal Medicine* 141. 5 (April 1981): 691-92.

Smith, Ronald E., M.D. and Robert A. Nozik, M.D. *Uveitis: A Clinical Approach to Diagnosis and Management.* Baltimore and London: Williams and Wilkins, 1983.

Spink, Wesley W., M.D. *Infectious Diseases—Prevention and Treatment in the Nineteenth and Twentieth Centuries.* Minneapolis: U of Minnesota P, 1978.

Sullivan, Edmund, M.D. "Ocular History of James Joyce." *Survey of Ophthalmology* 28. 5 (March/April 1984): 412-15.

Syphilis: A Synopsis. U.S. Dept. of Health, Education, and Welfare. Washington, D. C.: U. S. GPO, 1967.

Walsh, F.R., M.D. "New Light on James Joyce's Medical Problems." *Irish Medical Times* (9 May 1975).

Index